DECEMBER 8, 1980
THE DAY JOHN LENNON DIED

KEITH ELLIOT GREENBERG

Backbeat
Books

An Imprint of Hal Leonard Corporation

Published in 2010 by Backbeat Books
An Imprint of Hal Leonard Corporation
7777 West Bluemound Road
Milwaukee, WI 53213

Trade Book Division Editorial Offices
33 Plymouth St., Montclair, NJ 07042

Printed in the United States of America

Book design by UB Communications

Library of Congress Cataloging-in-Publication Data is available upon request.

ISBN 978-0-87930-963-3

www.backbeatbooks.com

To Jennifer

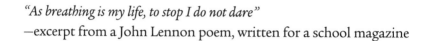

"As breathing is my life, to stop I do not dare"
—excerpt from a John Lennon poem, written for a school magazine

CONTENTS

1

BEEN SO LONG SINCE WE TOOK THE TIME

Below the high gables and terracotta spandrels—and the carved Lakota Indian gazing upon the yellow cabs and subway-bound commuters on Seventy-second Street—John Lennon scuttled around the Dakota, writing small notes to himself. Even with an album climbing on the charts, the former Beatle had grown to define himself as a house husband, and if he didn't make these scribblings, certain workaday tasks just wouldn't get done. With a five-year-old child at home, John and Yoko were awake at 8:00 A.M., planning the day and eating breakfast. At age forty, Lennon felt relatively healthy, renouncing the alcoholic tears that had characterized his youth in Liverpool and the Beatles' early days in Hamburg, as well as the fifteen-month "Lost Weekend" that nearly broke up his marriage. Among some rock 'n' rollers who'd grown up on the Beatles, forming a cocaine dependency ranked among the better ways to transition from the seventies to the eighties. But, having snorted his share in more thoughtless times, John now abstained.

Officially, John had also given up sugar. In the studio, though, he allowed himself to give in to arguably his most innocent of vices. John and Yoko had gone through a vegetarian phase and now aspired to be macrobiotic, eating whole grains and fish with rice. On a recent visit to the Dakota, however, an interviewer from *Playboy* had noticed that John still loved his Gauloises Bleues, the strong French cigarettes particularly popular in the Middle East.

"Macrobiotic people don't believe in the Big C," Lennon told the magazine, conceding that he was more than conscious of the possibility that he was deluding himself. "Macrobiotics don't believe that smoking is bad for you. Of course, if we die, we're wrong."

Mortality was an issue that came up often with Lennon. As a performer, he'd encouraged his listeners to abandon the parochial concept of earning a spot in heaven. Yet, without that secure notion to soothe him, he seemed to worry about his life ending prematurely. In virtually every interview, he broached the topic of death—even if it was to emphasize that he hoped to live a long, fulfilling life.

For more than a decade, the man who'd once smacked around insubordinate girlfriends and insolent associates had characterized himself as a pacifist. If someone challenged him to a fight, he said, he'd run away—shouting over his shoulder about peace. But Lennon pointed out that Mahatma Gandhi and Martin Luther King, Jr., had also forsaken violence—and been killed nonetheless.

In 1975, he'd removed himself from the public eye, spending the majority of his time in the warren of apartments the Lennons owned in the Dakota, the landmarked, North German Renaissance-style building on Central Park West—to live, not as a hermit, but as a civilian. The experience invigorated Lennon after years as a captive to fame. Even after the Beatles' breakup, John had felt like he couldn't escape his celebrity. And he'd believed that he had to hustle to maintain it—because, as much as he condemned the recording industry, he wanted to live up to the standards expected of Beatle John. During his five-year sabbatical from the business, he told one reporter, the "invisible ghost" had disappeared.

John's first marriage had occurred just as Beatlemania was launching in the United Kingdom, and drugs, groupies, and celebrity—coupled with the lessons Lennon had learned from his own dysfunctional parents—undermined the union from the beginning. The ex-Beatle's oldest son, Julian, was seventeen now, on the verge of a music career of his own. But only recently had Lennon been able to pull himself away from the complications of being a pop star to relate to the teen as a father in a council flat in Manchester, or a row house in Baltimore, would relate to a son. Years of bad feelings had yet to be addressed. When John discovered in early 1975 that forty-two-year-old Yoko had become pregnant with his second child, he vowed to undo the mistakes of the past.

Without the pressure of having to pay the rent every month, John could stay at home and place his complete focus on his youngest son, Sean. Despite what others believed, this decision did not mean that John had subjugated his personality. He followed music—New Wave, reggae, even disco—and wrote music, and cared about causes. But when Mick Jagger wanted to go out, John stayed inside.

It was better for the family.

If anyone didn't understand, John and Yoko's new album, *Double Fantasy*, was there to explain it all.

The release was a coup for record executive David Geffen, who'd recently signed the former Beatle—along with Elton John and Donna Summer—to his new Warner Brothers custom label, Geffen Records. As with John, Geffen's less than auspicious beginnings—his parents were refugees from British-mandated Palestine, and his mother owned a corset store in the Hasidic Jewish enclave of Borough Park in Brooklyn—created the drive to overtake the children of privilege as well as the ability to read, and even challenge, the tastes of the record-buying public. However, *Double Fantasy* was a distant leap from such abstract offerings as "Glass Onion," "I Am the Walrus," and "Revolution 9." No longer was John attempting to mess with listeners' minds; his goal was communicating with them directly. The songs expressed the simplicity of the life the Lennons tried creating in the Dakota, celebrating kinship, romance, and childhood.

More significantly, Lennon maintained, he didn't have to repackage himself to compete with Elvis Costello or the Cars. His authentic personality—and the emotions he expressed through his music—were enough.

With the release of the album, John seemed to swing open the doors to the Dakota, inviting the press—and the world—back into his sphere. John's fans appeared happy to be there; in just three weeks, *Double Fantasy* had sold 700,000 copies. "(Just Like) Starting Over," the former Beatle's first single since 1975, had been released not because of its marketing potential, but because its premise—going home again, and moving forward—best expressed his current attitude. On December 8, 1980, it was #3 in the United States.

■　■　■

In the past, John Lennon had rarely allowed himself to feel satisfied with his work, complaining about the quality of his songs. Once, when George Martin—the Beatles' storied producer—assured the performer that his music was treasured, John retorted, "Well, if I could do them all over again, I would."

This form of discontent seemed to follow John into every endeavor, the agitation fueling his creativity yet arresting his ability to enjoy the world around him. But the happier John Lennon fans were meeting on *Double Fantasy* had not sacrificed any of his artistic edge. Indeed, his art seemed to have acquired a new dimension. Although willing to bare his pain when necessary, he could also rejoice. As the name of his first single suggested, he was starting fresh—personally and professionally. In his mind, all that history—the Beatles; the self-destructive, rock star behavior; the U.S. government's efforts to deport him—were wiped clean. "I feel like nothing has ever happened before today," he told the RKO radio network.

Now, switching on a tape recorder, John listened to a rough mix of "Walking on Thin Ice," the dance song Yoko was in the process of refining at the Record Plant, the West Forty-fourth Street studio where he'd recorded *Imagine* in 1971. Founder Gary

Kellgren's goal had always been establishing a studio that felt less like the fluorescent-lit laboratories where records were usually churned out, and more like a living room in the musician's home. The concept had been a successful one. Jimi Hendrix's *Electric Ladyland*, Bruce Springsteen's *Born to Run*, KISS's *Destroyer*, and Aerosmith's *Toys in the Attic* had all been germinated in the Record Plant. It was there that John and Yoko had already laid down the demo tracks for an album of songs that hadn't made it onto *Double Fantasy*. There were discussions about an album after that, as well. After five years in exile, the couple was contemplating a world tour.

John knew that this would mean swarming hordes; sycophants; tired, cranky musicians; and promoters with questionable scruples. But he was a performer, and needed to feel the energy of a live concert again. It would be different than in the past. The relationship with Sean had matured John Lennon. If any adolescent peculiarities lingered, Yoko would be there to impose order. Another type of man would rebel against a wife who set clear limits. But John sought structure from the woman he openly called "Mother," and had once described not only as an equal, but "my better, actually."

In addition to contributing to John's music, "Mother" had multiplied his personal fortune. In 1980, John was earning approximately $12 million in annual royalties, but his portfolio was worth some $235 million, due to his wife's investing in, among other ventures, 250 Holstein Friesian cattle, the world's highest production dairy animal, worth more than $66 million; a total of four dairy farms in Vermont, Virginia, and Delaware County, New York; two estates in Yoko's native Japan; and homes in Palm Beach, Laurel Canyon, and the old whaling village of Cold Spring Harbor, on Long Island. The self-professed "working class hero" made no apologies for amassing this windfall, since each year the couple made it a point to donate ten percent of their income to charity.

Ten years earlier, when the Lennons moved into the Dakota, neighbors had been concerned about the element they'd attract to the gloomy, soot-stained building. The nine-story structure, with its haunting Gothic details, already enjoyed a certain degree of notoriety—Roman Polanski had chosen to film *Rosemary's Baby* there, and prior residents included the cinematic Frankenstein, Boris Karloff, as well as the tragic Judy Garland. Still, John's neighbors were touchy about who shared the building's airy corridors or passed through the black, wrought-iron gates—fearing the sight of unruly paparazzi crushing cigarette butts against the helmeted gargoyles and serpents wrapped around the cooperative's heavy black railing.

When the Lennons first sublet actor Robert Ryan's apartment—on the seventh floor, overlooking Central Park—neighbors were surprised that the former Beatle and his spouse sought the same type of privacy as everyone else. There were neither parties nor complaints. By the time John and Yoko were ready to purchase in 1973—they'd end up buying up twenty-five rooms in five apartments—the pair was not only tolerated, but embraced. Every year, Yoko prepared a Japanese feast for the entire building, providing chopsticks, as she played with her son and quietly chatted with John or her friend and fellow resident Lauren Bacall—who, on December 8, 1980, had recently finished filming *The Fan*, a thriller about a stage actress being stalked by a homicidal admirer.

2

THIS IS MY STATEMENT

As New Yorkers rode to work on subways and buses on the morning of December 8, 1980—turning past the ads in the tabloids for Mays and Alexander's department stores, Eastern Airlines, and current movies like *Raging Bull* and *Private Benjamin*—they learned that Ronald Reagan—elected to the White House the month before—and his wife, Nancy, were about to fly into the city. Reagan's plans included a meeting with the Catholic cardinal of New York, Terrence Cooke, and lunch with the youngest member of the Reagan family, Ron Prescott Reagan. The future first couple had apparently been taken by surprise when the twenty-two-year-old ballet dancer suddenly married his live-in girlfriend, Doria Palmieri, and the elder Reagan hoped to engage his son in a private chat. The groom's mother announced that she would not be joining the two at lunch.

After enduring the Vietnam War, the Watergate Affair, and the televised images of those whooping "students" in Tehran burning the Stars and Stripes and effigies of President Jimmy Carter while fifty-two Americans remained imprisoned in the U.S. embassy, America was a battered land. A day earlier, Iran had marked the 400th day of the hostage crisis with wild celebration. Conscious of the discomfort his dour, black-turbanned countenance caused in American living rooms, eighty-year-old Ayatollah Ruhollah Khomeini hailed his Islamic revolution as a "conquest of hearts," and urged his followers to export the movement to other countries.

After four years of the ethically sound but delicate Jimmy Carter, Reagan—the former cinematic cowboy—was seen in some quarters as the new sheriff in town, the pistol twirler the nation needed to induce fear in both the swirl-eyed, bearded Islamic fundamentalists and those insidious Reds in the Soviet Union. And, to his exponents, his ascension couldn't have come at a more opportune time. Almost a year to the day that the Soviets invaded Afghanistan, the long-feared confrontation between East and West appeared to be on the horizon. On December 7, the lame-duck Carter White House had exasperatedly declared that—while he was overwhelmed by the humiliation in Iran—there were indications that between 300,000 and 400,000 Soviet troops, backed by East German and Czechoslovakian units, were ready to roll across the border into Poland. In the Vatican, Pope John Paul II commemorated the Feast of the Immaculate Conception by praying to the Blessed Virgin to protect the nation of his birth.

"I cannot help but speak as a son of Poland of my beloved homeland," the Pontiff said. "The news which comes out of Poland is very alarming. We all hope it will not turn out to be true."

While the Catholic Church was warring with forces on the left in Central Europe, in Central America, the liberation theology wing of the faith was colliding with right-wing governments traditionally supported by the United States. Less than a week earlier, the bodies of nuns Ita Ford and Maura Clarke from New York City and Dorothy Kazel from Cleveland, as well as a religious social worker, Jean Donovan, also from Cleveland, had been discovered beside a rural road in El Salvador. During Sunday Mass at San Salvador's Metropolitan Cathedral, Bishop Arturo Rivera y Damas blamed "the persecution of the church and specifically the assassination of . . . church agents on the security forces and ultra-rightist gangs. And, consequently, we blame the governing junta."

In response to the controversy, the Carter administration cut off military and economic assistance to El Salvador. But observers were curious about how Reagan—who believed the fight against communism took precedence over other ideological concerns—would alter the country's Central American policy.

John Lennon liked Jimmy Carter, and was more sensitive to the crimes of U.S.-supported military goons than to those of communists and Shia Muslims. In the midst of his protest phase, he might have joined the leftovers from the hippie and yippie movements, gathering downtown in Union Square Park to brand the president-elect a demagogue. But John had mellowed, Reagan won his election with authority, and the United States was taking a decidedly conservative turn.

John said little about Central America, just as he refrained from agitating for ten hunger-striking Irish Republican Army (IRA) inmates in Northern Ireland. Like many natives of Liverpool—where the Everton Football Club was once known as the city's Irish Catholic team—John could trace his roots, and eccentricities, to the Emerald Isle. His 1972 album, *Some Time in New York City*, included two songs championing the severing of Northern Ireland's six counties from British rule: "Sunday Bloody Sunday" (not to be confused with the U2 tune also written about the slaughter of twenty-seven civil rights demonstrators in Derry, Northern Ireland) and "The Luck of the Irish," a track rife with references to a millennium of "torture and hunger," and to "British brigands" committing rape and genocide. But, with the release of *Double Fantasy*, John was steering away from the volatile topic.

In New York—where one in every fifty Caucasian citizens was genetically linked to Niall of the Nine Hostages, the fifth-century Irish high king—the state's officials could not afford to be as quiet. Senator Alfonse D'Amato was currently in Northern Ireland, meeting with the hunger strikers' families. Mayor Ed Koch also expressed sympathy for the Irish rebels, periodically reminding constituents that Irish-American New Yorkers were more consistently loyal to him than his fellow Jews.

Koch was fond of listening to the Beatles in the mayoral car. Although he was partial to Paul McCartney's songwriting and musical fare, the mayor personally liked John Lennon, and appreciated that the former Beatle had chosen to make New York his town. In Koch's words, the sight of Lennon "gave cheer" to neighbors, pedestrians, and shop owners: "New York City appeals to everyone who wants to take advantage of anonymity. People are respectful of one another's privacy. You can be famous and walk around, and people won't intrude."

Tall and balding, with an alternately jokey and prickly demeanor, Koch was a Greenwich Village bachelor who'd demonstrated for civil rights and against the Vietnam War. By the time he ran for mayor in 1977, he'd begun describing himself as a "liberal with sanity," taking a tough, law-and-order approach that appealed to blue-collar voters in places like Bay Ridge, Brooklyn and Woodside, Queens. When Reagan was running for president, Koch invited him to Gracie Mansion, angering onetime supporters who viewed the gesture as an endorsement of the conservative Republican. Likewise, the mayor's decision to save the city money by closing Sydenham Hospital in Harlem—one of the few local institutions with a significant percentage of African-American doctors—provoked charges of racism, and insensitivity to the needs of the black community. Nonetheless, in late 1980, the mayor still enjoyed a great deal of popularity. When he'd wade through a crowd, shouting "How'm I doing?" the response was usually positive.

The golden moment of his mayoralty had arguably occurred in April, when bus and subway operators went on strike and Koch pushed back, walking across the Brooklyn Bridge and shaking hands with commuters striding to their offices in Manhattan.

"No question about it," he later remembered. "The people of New York City said to the illegal strikers, 'Fuck you. We're going to walk all over you.' Oh, it was wonderful. It was New York's finest hour."

Like the Lennon of old, Koch took great pride in holding a grudge. In 1965, he'd crossed party lines to endorse the former mayor, John V. Lindsay. When Lindsay later endorsed a Koch opponent, the enmity began. "I did not have a high regard for John Lindsay," Koch said. "I didn't think he was smart. I didn't think he was appreciative of what I'd done for him. He was responsible for spending money we didn't have. He caused, in great part, financial problems I had to deal with."

Upon his own election, Koch gleefully attacked his predecessor whenever the opportunity arose. Lindsay asked a mutual friend to intercede. "He wanted me to stop berating him," Koch said. "Otherwise, he would have to leave town—he was so overwhelmed by my comments."

Eventually, Koch agreed to a backhanded compromise, pledging never to mention John Lindsay again. "When I need to refer to him," the mayor promised, "I will call him Mayor X."

■   ■   ■

Ellen Chesler worked down the hall from the mayor, as chief of staff for Carol Bellamy, the city council president and future UNICEF head—and the first female ever elected to citywide office. She'd also been living downstairs from John Lennon for the past three years.

An American historian, Chesler had first visited the Dakota for an event in Betty Friedan's apartment. Friedan, a cofounder of the National Organization for Women (NOW) and America's most noted feminist, added to the bohemian quality of the building, and Chesler was charmed. "There were a lot of interesting, artistic people in the Dakota," she said. "The building wasn't clean. It was little rundown and old. But the architecture was fantastic." When a cheap apartment became available in 1977, Chesler and her attorney husband moved in.

According to local folklore, the Dakota had been named after distant Dakota Territory, due to its status as the first high rise in the remote reaches a mile or so north of midtown. But since this tale didn't appear in the press until 1933, a half-century after the Dakota's construction, it's more likely that the developer had simply intended to honor the expanding American west. In 1980, before, in Chesler's words, the structure was "chic'd up" and marketed to investment bankers, socially conscious residents with modest incomes were accustomed to sharing the elevator with the Lennons, Bacall, conductor Leonard Bernstein, and singer Roberta Flack. "There were just great people there," Chesler said, "a filmmaker, an antiques dealer. The kids played together in the courtyard and the internal stairwells. It was a wonderful community. My children loved growing up there."

A native Ohioan, Chesler had seen the Beatles perform at Cleveland's Municipal Stadium in 1964. As soon as John, Paul, George, and Ringo set foot on stage, the fans surged forward, spilling out of the grandstand onto the ballfield and trampling one another. Chesler remembered the situation becoming so unmanageable that, after a few songs, the concert came to an abrupt halt, and the Beatles were suddenly evacuated from the stadium.

When they returned two years later, the Beatles were brought to the stage in an armored truck. Once again, though, the fans were uncontrollable, knocking down the fence and storming the stage. In the middle of the performance, the Beatles were shoved back into their armored truck, and spectators were told that the group would leave if order were not restored. Grudgingly, the fans returned to their seats and—after a forty-five-minute break—the show resumed.

Chesler was too urbane to approach John and bring up her memories about the Beatles' visits to C-Town. Sean Lennon was always an exuberant, friendly presence in the building. But his parents kept their distance, and Chesler and her husband understood why.

"I don't want to be too blasé about it," she said. "John Lennon was John Lennon."

■   ■   ■

One mile south of the Dakota, another person who venerated Lennon was preparing for what would become the biggest day in his life.

At about 11:00 A.M., twenty-five-year-old Mark David Chapman, a nondescript, slightly pudgy visitor from Honolulu, awoke in the Sheraton Hotel and slipped on his spectacles. Though the sun made the day seem uncharacteristically warm for Christmas season, there was a moderate wind rolling down Seventh Avenue from Central Park, and Chapman dressed carefully, aware that he'd be spending long hours outside. Beneath his tan sweater, he insulated his body with a thermal undershirt. Then he slipped on a pair of conservative, dark blue slacks, and brown suede shoes.

Chapman had a sense that he wouldn't be coming back that night. So he laid out a number of items for police to find, among them a leather Bible. He turned to the Gospel of John, grabbed a pen, and changed the wording: "The Gospel of John Lennon."

The visitor reached for his favorite book, *The Catcher in the Rye*, about an alienated teen waging a battle in his mind against "phonies." He cracked open the shiny red cover and wrote, "This is my statement," signing it with the name of the book's protagonist, Holden Caulfield.

■　■　■

At the height of their fame, the Beatles often felt caged inside their hotels as hysterical hordes screeched outside their windows and handlers acted as intermediaries to the outside world. During earlier times in New York, John had been nervous about turning his back on groups of aficionados, concerned that one might grab a handful of hair—in the old days, fans attempted to snip the Beatles' signature locks with scissors—or knock him over with a powerful hug. But today John was more relaxed, and conscious that he and his admirers shared the city together. It seemed like the fans could read his signals and approach him with respect. Consequently, John enjoyed acknowledging rather than running from the public.

"I've been walking these streets for the last seven years," he told BBC Radio. "I can go right out this door now and go to a restaurant.

You want to know how great that is? Or go to the movies. I mean, people come up and ask for autographs or say 'hi,' but they won't bug you."

Before their macrobiotic phase, John and Yoko would suddenly appear on the Lower East Side, grabbing a table in Ratner's, an ancient kosher dairy restaurant, ordering blintzes from cranky, Yiddish-accented waiters. Near the Dakota, John was a regular at Hisae's, sometimes taking home a vegetable and fish dish, or a piece of chocolate cake baked—in keeping with the macrobiotic creed—with honey rather than sugar.

As a full-time father, John was regularly sighted walking hand-in-hand with Sean into the pediatrician's office and sitting down to read a newspaper or magazine in the waiting room, among the other parents. Despite the flurry of activity generated by the Lennons' numerous assistants, John would also seek out quiet places at home where he could teach his son to draw, write, and read.

In 1979, John and Yoko attempted to describe their choices to fans in an advertisement in the *New York Times*, headlined "A Love Letter From John and Yoko. To People Who Ask Us What, When and Why." The dispatch told of the couple's appreciation of family living, and of the city that was versatile enough to allow them to function on their own terms:

"The house is getting very comfortable now. Sean is beautiful. The plants are growing. The cats are purring. The town is shining, sun, rain or snow."

Most importantly, the pair stressed, the departure from public life was anything but a rejection of the people who cared about them and their music.

"If you think of us," the letter underscored, "remember our silence is a silence of love and not of indifference."

Certainly, the Lennons were not indifferent to New York City.

They arranged for Sean, at three and a half, to visit Hale House, a Harlem home for infants and toddlers of drug-addicted mothers.

John and Yoko also sent food and clothing to the children, along with a check for $10,000.

On Thanksgiving, the couple donated 1,200 packages of fresh fruit, raisins, and nuts, as well as woolly scarves, to the needy. John and Yoko also made sure that thousands of gift baskets were allocated to the elderly too infirm to leave their homes, and to youthful offenders confined to the Spofford House of Detention in the Bronx.

"In this day of Thanksgiving," an accompanying note read, "we are thinking of you, and we wish you a happy life.... Love, John, Yoko and Sean."

When John's friend, photographer Bob Gruen, wanted to depict Lennon in the environment where he felt most at ease, the former Beatle was positioned on a rooftop, with the Manhattan skyline behind him, wearing a T-shirt with the words "New York City" inscribed across his chest.

Although eternally proud of his Liverpudlian accent and heritage, John loved New York with the affection one could only associate with home. It was a place, John said, where "there is no harassment." A place where the former Beatle and his family felt safe.

3

CAN'T EXPLAIN SO MUCH PAIN

Paul McCartney enjoyed his solitude.

At his Sussex estate, he often left the television and radio off and disconnected the phone at night. Like John—the man he'd cursed, battled, and loved, as if he were a brother—Paul didn't mind drawing the blinds on the outside world and savoring the pleasure of just being around his family. If there was something important to do, Paul was disciplined enough to remember it. On December 8, he was thinking about a meeting he'd arranged with George Martin, the Beatles' former producer. The two were working together again, on Paul's next album.

Among Beatle devotees, there were various factions. One blamed the group's breakup on Yoko's intrusion into the Fab Four. Another diminished Paul as too mainstream for the avant-garde Lennon, and too overbearing to allow consensus within the band. Although McCartney had developed a thick skin, he was acutely aware of the criticisms. Yet he could take comfort in the fact that, over the past decade, he'd experienced the greatest success of all the Beatles.

Despite his consistent string of albums, George Harrison hadn't played a live show since 1976. After a spurt of early hits, Ringo Starr's solo triumphs were uneven. And John, of course, had gone on sabbatical in 1975.

By contrast, since 1971, Paul's new band, Wings—cofounded with Denny Laine, the Moody Blues' former guitarist and lead singer—had flourished. Every one of the twenty-three singles released by the band had ended up on the American Top 40 charts. Still, it had been a trying year for the group, beginning in January, when Paul was busted coming into Tokyo with nearly half a pound of marijuana (the conspiracy theorists among Beatles buffs hypothesized that Yoko was the one who'd tipped off authorities in her birthplace). After nine days behind bars, Paul was deported; he wouldn't return to the country for another decade.

When Wings next convened, they began writing songs and distilling unreleased older tracks. Since October, they'd been laboring at George Martin's Air Studios on Oxford Street in London, attempting to put together their ninth album.

Paul was confident about the project. After all, just the year before, "Coming Up" had become the group's sixth #1 hit in the U.S. In fact, Paul's post-Beatle eminence was so absolute that some believed John had specifically wanted to humble him when he released *Double Fantasy*.

McCartney didn't doubt it.

There had always been competition between the two, from the moment Paul spotted sixteen-year-old John—in a checkered shirt and pompadour—on stage in the garden of St. Peter's Woolton Parish Church, singing "Be-Bop-A-Lula."

Paul initially thought that Lennon was affecting a sneer behind the microphone—not realizing that John was so nearsighted that just focusing on the audience was a chore. After the set, Paul introduced himself and—in a harbinger of things to come—began correcting his future partner. McCartney tuned John's guitar—a skill Lennon had not been able to master—before writing down the proper lyrics for "Be-Bop-A-Lula" and Eddie Cochran's "Twenty Flight Rock."

Both Lennon and McCartney had genetic predispositions for music. Paul's grandfather Joe—not to be confused with Wilfrid Brambell, who'd portray the Beatle's angry Irish granddad in *A Hard Day's Night*—played the E-flat tuba. In the 1920s, Paul's father, Jim, fronted Jim Mac's Jazz Band. In the McCartney home, Jim played the trumpet and upright piano—a purchase from the music store owned by future Beatles manager Brian Epstein's family—and taught his son how to identify various instruments by listening to them on the radio.

Paul wanted to play the guitar, but found it difficult. He was left-handed, and couldn't quite get the right sound from the nylon strings. It was only when Paul saw a poster of fellow lefty Slim Whitman—whose country song, "Rose Marie," sat at the top of the British charts in 1955—that he came up with a way to configure the strings in the opposite direction.

For some reason—perhaps the Celtic and British folk underpin-nings of Appalachian melodies—Whitman and his C&W peers had had a significant impact on the English music scene; Ringo Starr, at one point, had even played drums in a band called the Raving Texans. In 1956, skiffle hit the UK, blending American folk and blues with jazz. The genre—made famous by Lonnie Donegan, the East London–reared son of a Scottish violinist—relied on a basic, three-chord style, and within a span of months, teenage skiffle groups had sprouted everywhere from Brighton to Aberdeen.

With his mother, Julia's encouragement, John—then a student at Quarry Bank Grammar School, the equivalent of a high school—formed his own band, called the Quarrymen, a tongue-in-cheek tribute to the lyrics of the school song ("Quarry men, strong before their birth"). After Paul joined the group, they went through a number of incarnations, calling themselves the Beetles—in deference to, depending on the story, the all-girl gang of the same name in the Marlon Brando film *The Wild Ones*, or Buddy Holly's band, the Crickets—the Silver Beetles, and, ultimately, the Beatles.

The name was John's idea, a playful reference to the beat music that succeeded skiffle in Britain's industrial north. Lennon would later joke that he'd seen a vision of a flaming pie in the air, proclaiming, "You are Beatles with an 'A.'"

Of all the people in Lennon's life at the time, his mother under-stood his roguish wit best. Both Julia and John were artistic and felt estranged from proper society—disparaging the rigid people who judged them as "thickheads." Julia loved a good practical joke, deliberately wearing spectacles without glass, then reaching through the frame to rub her eye. Despite what was expected of women of her generation, the effervescent redhead appeared unashamed of her sensuality—and of the fact that she'd had two daughters out of wedlock with her boyfriend, Bobby Dykins—and boasted of her great aversion to household chores, doing a parody of a ballet dance while dusting.

Because Julia's family questioned her parenting skills, John lived with his mother's sister, Mimi, for much of his childhood. But his visits to Julia's home were memorable. On at least one occasion, she entertained John's friends by sweeping the floor with a pair of women's underwear on her head, the legs of the old-fashioned bloomers dangling around her neck.

John loved her more than anyone in the world. Then, on July 15, 1958, he was sitting in her home with John Dykins when a policeman knocked on the door.

"Are you Julia's son?" the officer asked.

"Yes, I am."

"I'm sorry to have to tell you this. But your mother's been killed."

Julia had run into John's friend, Nigel Whalley, outside Mimi's house. Since the two were walking in the same direction, they strolled down Menlove Avenue, exchanging jokes and laughing, until Julia said goodbye and Nigel turned up Vale Road, toward his home.

He'd walked about fifteen yards before he heard a car skidding and then a thud. When Nigel spun around, he was astonished to see the body of his friend's mother flying through the air for about a hundred feet before crashing to the ground.

Julia had been struck by a Standard Vanguard car driven by off-duty police officer Eric Clague. "Mrs. Lennon just ran straight out in front of me," he later insisted. "I just couldn't avoid her. I was not speeding. I swear it. It was just one of those terrible things that can happen."

The official cause of death: brain injuries caused by skull fractures.

From John's point of view, though, there was no making sense of why the forty-four-year-old free spirit had been stolen from him so abruptly. "I can't explain so much pain," he sang in 1970. "My mummy's dead."

"I lost her twice," John would tell *Playboy* magazine, "when I was five and I moved in with my auntie, and then when she physically died. That made me more bitter. The chip on my shoulder I had as a youth got really big then. I was just really re-establishing the relationship with her, and she was killed."

■   ■   ■

Although they'd often clash and razz each other, Lennon and McCartney shared a painful connection. Some eight months before the two met, Paul had lost his own mother, Mary, a midwife, from an embolism following a mastectomy. Although Paul didn't bare his agony the way his partner did, he also named a child after his mother, and referred to "Mother Mary" as a comforting figure in "Let It Be." Later, each would become close enough to his respective wife to incorporate her into his band—an indication, perhaps, that both Beatles needed assurance that the women they now loved could always be found, standing behind them.

Paul's father had warned him that John could get him "into trouble." And with Lennon as a friend, the academically inclined McCartney began to turn his attention away from school, repairing to his empty home while his father was out to write songs. This was unusual for two teenagers in Britain, where the majority of pop stars either re-recorded American hits or performed tunes written by established composers. At the beginning, at least, Paul was more musically astute and a better storyteller, while John was willing to reveal torment and anger, singing in a raw Liverpudlian accent rather than mimicking American vocal traits.

To be certain, both boys were influenced by African-American performers like Little Richard and Sam Cooke, embedding in the pair an abiding a respect for many elements of black culture in the United States. Yet, even as they integrated American rhythms and melodies, Lennon and McCartney quickly perfected a style unique to them. It was the power and sincerity in John's voice, many believed, that gave the Beatles the energy that distinguished them from their competitors. And even though Paul and George were better musicians, John's rapid-fire playing—along with his tender fingerwork—added to the passion and intricacy of the performance.

Sometimes Paul wrote the first part of a song, and John added a section. Other times, they would share credit for songs one or the other had written on his own. Believing that they could become stars, the two always concentrated on a marketable hook. But while Paul was generally content with hopeful, romantic lyrics, John focused on the reasons that the singer was expressing a particular sentiment.

Noted John, "You could say that [Paul] provided a lightness and optimism, while I would always go for the sadness, the discords, a certain bluesy edge."

Yet, Paul would maintain that the notion that he was only capable of gentle fare, while John was the hard-rocking cynic, was an oversimplified "fallacy." Although much has been written about John's malicious humor, Paul occasionally teased John about his mother's unconventional living arrangements, and Linda McCartney later admitted that her husband could display an unpleasant "hard edge" at home. Paul also conceded that he'd bossed John around.

In 1980, with the bitterness associated with the Beatles' breakup receding into history, both John and Paul were able to acknowledge the other's talents. John spoke about Paul's bass playing as innovative and underrated. "He is an egomaniac about everything else about himself," Lennon told *Playboy*. "But his bass playing, he was always a bit coy about." Like the undervalued Ringo, John continued, Paul was at the top of his class: "As pure musicians, as inspired humans to make the noise, they are as good as anybody."

For his part, Paul compared John to Elvis. "I always idolized him," McCartney contended.

■   ■   ■

With a copy of *Double Fantasy* under his arm, Mark David Chapman exited his hotel room, an experience he'd compare to passing through a giant portal, with his past left on the other side.

In his words, he was "a runaway train...not anything could have stopped me."

This was not the first time Chapman had become fixated on a celebrity. In a Larry King interview, he recalled the time he'd learned that Leslie Nielsen and Robert Goulet were attending an opening at an art gallery, and rushed to the location. Goulet had been in the middle of a conversation when Chapman tapped him from behind, and turned wondering why this guy had just interrupted the discussion.

Chapman had been too narcissistic to care about protocol. He asked Goulet to pose for a photo with him, and the onetime Broadway actor acquiesced, even managing a smile. Chapman felt important being in this environment. But as soon as he left the gallery, he'd recall, his self-esteem evaporated.

In truth, there was little reason to feel this way. In Hawaii, Chapman had a sweet-natured wife who loved him despite his ramblings, depression, and paranoia. A born-again Christian, he'd enjoyed the fellowship of others with similar beliefs at different times, and could have opened the phone book and discovered dozens of New York churches where he'd find sympathy and support. Without question, the members would have relieved him of the revolver he'd purchased six weeks earlier for $169, and—in those days when airport security was more lax—carried back and forth to New York twice in the past month.

The .38-caliber Charter Arms Undercover Special was a favorite with off-duty cops, its snub-nosed frame slightly smaller than the Smith & Wesson generally issued to police officers. In order to penetrate a human body, a bullet needed to travel at least 300 feet per second. Chapman's gun could fire five rounds at between 700 and 750. But timing and positioning were crucial. Chapman wanted his encounter with Lennon to bring him immortality. If the assassin missed his target, his name would slip out of the headlines in a few short days—particularly in New York, where several other crime stories were receiving prominent play.

Just that morning, the trial of Jean Harris had been featured in the local dailies. Harris—the patrician former headmistress at the exclusive Madeira School for Girls, outside Washington, D.C.—was on trial north of the city, in White Plains, for murdering her lover, Herman Tarnower, author of *The Complete Scarsdale Medical Diet*.

The day before, Detective Arthur Siciliano had told the court that the accused shooter confided, "I loved him very much. I've been through so much hell with him. He slept with every woman he could, and I'd had it."

In July, between acts of the Berlin Ballet at the Metropolitan Opera, a Canadian farm girl whose passion for the violin had drawn her to New York and the Juilliard School of Music, had left her instrument on her chair. When she didn't return, fellow members of the orchestra notified security. The next day, her nude body was found, bound and gagged, at the bottom of an air shaft. It seemed like a mystery out of a Hitchcock film, and fifty detectives were enlisted to interview 300 performers and employees. Eventually, they arrested Craig Stephen Crimmins, a twenty-one-year-old stagehand from New Jersey, accusing him of attempting to rape the thirty-one-year-old violinist on the roof of the opera house before throwing her down the shaft.

On December 8, 1980, the suspect's coworkers at the Met, along with his childhood friends, gathered up $50,000 and bailed him out of jail. "There were a lot of tears all over the place," Crimmins told the *New York Post.* "I just sat and waited, day in and day out, knowing that one day I'd be out, and I'd be able to prove my innocence."

By the time Crimmins was convicted of murder in June 1981, no one cared.

Everybody was still talking about Mark David Chapman.

4

Not Afraid to Be Afraid

One of the most touching tracks on *Double Fantasy* was "Beautiful Boy," a father's gentle song about his love for his young son. This was not the first time that John's fans had listened, as he opened his heart. With "Beautiful Boy," he was revealing what may have been his reason to live.

"I can hardly wait to see you come of age," John sang of Sean's long journey toward manhood. "But I guess we'll both just have to be patient."

Yoko's voice was also featured, reminding Sean not to hold back his tears or turn away from his true emotions. These were the words not of an entertainer mouthing an interesting lyric, but of a mother supporting her son, reassuring him that he didn't have to swagger and posture to gain affirmation—because he'd always have his parents' unconditional caring.

It was an ethic so different from the one John and his peers had ingested. Back in Liverpool, boys were socialized to believe that it was better to pretend to be tough—even if that meant that you bullied females and provoked violence with other males—than to be perceived as weak.

But that was a long time ago in the evolution of John Lennon. "I'm not afraid to be afraid," he'd recently told *Rolling Stone*, "though it's always scary. But it's more painful not to be yourself."

Through all the trials that Sean would face in life, the song was John's eternal gift to his child—the voice of his father reminding him not to worry because everything was always going to be okay.

Sean could listen to John explaining the unfettered pleasure of holding his boy's hand as they crossed the street, protecting him not only from the traffic, but whatever else the youngest Lennon feared.

Nothing could have been more dissimilar from the way John Winston Lennon's own life began, on the second floor of the Oxford Street Maternity Hospital on October 9, 1940—with his father away at sea, and German bombs falling on England.

John's father, Alfred—alternately known as "Alf" or "Fred"—was the grandson of immigrants who came to Liverpool from County Down in Northern Ireland, likely descendents of the O'Leannain or O'Lonain clans. According to folklore, Alf's father, Jack, was a singer who toured the United States in the 1890s, performing in blackface as a Kentucky minstrel. The story isn't true—even though a musical strain was undoubtedly passed down through the generations. Like his future wife, Alf sang and played the banjo.

As a toddler, Alf developed rickets, which stunted his growth and forced him into heavy leg braces. To compensate, the cleft-chinned youngster entertained friends and relatives by doing imitations and telling stories. Even as an adult, he'd amuse acquaintances by singing like Louis Armstrong or Al Jolson, and regaling them with tales about his mother, Polly Maguire, who, although illiterate, could allegedly forecast the future by reading the messages in playing cards or tea leaves.

Like Julia Lennon later on, though, Polly would not be able to care for her child. When Jack Lennon died, Polly tried supporting her large family by taking in washing. Unfortunately, she had just too many kids and too many expenses. As a result, Alf and his sister, Edith—the two youngest children—were sent around the corner to Blue Coat School Orphanage.

It was a less than idyllic existence, and Alf didn't like taking orders, anyway. So in 1927, at age fifteen, he joined a children's music hall act, running away with the troupe. Remarkably, the orphanage sent representatives to find him. Evetunally, he was located in Glasgow, and forced to return to the children's asylum.

Once he came of age, Alf led a seafaring existence, signing up with the Merchant Navy, and working as a bellhop and steward on cruise ships.

Alf was fifteen when he first spotted fourteen-year-old Julia Stanley—the daughter of a middle-class family of Welsh extraction—but didn't speak to her until the opportunity presented itself. Julia was seated on a wrought-iron bench in Sefton Park, and had no place to flee when Alf approached, wielding a cigarette holder and sporting a bowler hat.

"You look silly," Julia said.

"And you look lovely," Alf replied, helping himself to a seat.

Julia shook her head. "Bugger off," she demanded.

Alf stayed put.

"Well, take the hat off, then."

Exhibiting the type of spontaneity for which his son would be renowned, Alf Lennon accommodated the request by grasping the brim of his bowler and hurling it into the lake.

The moment would come to represent the tone of the couple's relationship, even as they grew out of their teens—impulsive, mischievous, adversarial, immature.

The traits would feed John Lennon's angst and creativity, and define him until the beginnings of his *Double Fantasy* phase.

■   ■   ■

Julia and her family lived on Newcastle Road, close to the orphanage where Alf Lennon had been forced to reside. Because of the city's location on the River Mersey, many Liverpool men earned a living either on the docks or at sea, and Julia's father, George, was no exception. He differed from Alf Lennon, however, in that he never intended to remain on the ocean. As his family grew, George took a more sensible job, as an insurance adjuster for a salvage company, even purchasing a home in the suburbs.

The Stanleys ended up in a neat, terraced house in a section of Woolton known as Penny Lane.

From the beginning, the Stanleys detested Alf, believing that Julia was too young and too erratic to have a boyfriend, and that the young man was clearly below their station. At one stage, George Stanley tried finding Alf a job on a whaling ship, not because the elder man wished to assist his daughter's love interest, but because the tour would last two years—time enough, George reasoned, for Julia to find someone else.

Alf refused the job, and the relationship continued. In 1938, eleven years after their first meeting, Julia proposed to Alf Lennon.

The couple married in Liverpool's Bolton Street Register Office. Alf's brother Sydney was the best man at the brief ceremony. Not one member of Julia's family attended.

The couple repaired to Clayton Square for a celebratory meal at Reece's Restaurant, a slightly upscale eatery where the local branch of the Freemasons held meetings. After a trip to the movies, Alf went back to his rooming house, while Julia returned home, wedding certificate in hand.

"There!" she shouted at her father. "I married him!"

The next morning, Alf shipped out to the West Indies. He wouldn't return to Liverpool for three months.

■ ■ ■

After the birth of John, the Stanleys grudgingly allowed Alf to stay at their home during his visits back from the war front, where he was working as a merchant seaman on Britain's troop transport ships. For the first three years of John's life, Alf sent his paychecks to his wife. Then, in 1943, the money stopped arriving. Alf had gone AWOL.

On a certain level, the shared sense of abandonment bonded John and his mother. Julia took a job at a café near her son's school, dropping him off and picking him up each day. But at twenty-nine years old, Julia had needs that the boy couldn't fill.

Shortly before he vanished, Alf—perhaps knowing that he was about to turn away from his family—began writing letters encouraging Julia to go out and have a good time. She took him at his word and, by 1945, had met a Welsh soldier at a tearoom and become pregnant. The serviceman knew that he was having an affair with a woman who was still technically married, and now refused to move in with Julia unless she passed the remnant of that failed relationship—her son—on somewhere else.

Julia chose John instead.

Her family was aghast, and demanded that Julia put the infant up for adoption. In the midst of this calamity, Alf turned up in Liverpool, blaming himself for causing the situation, and offering to raise the child as his own.

Julia was no longer interested. She needed to sort out her life, and Alf wouldn't be much help. Ten days after the birth of her child, the little girl—eventually christened Lillian Ingrid Maria Pederson—was adopted by a Norwegian sailor and his wife.

Meanwhile, Alf attempted to re-establish his connection to John. In 1946, Alf took his son to Blackpool, a resort community on the Irish Sea, primarily for residents of British mill towns. When Julia learned that her husband planned to use Blackpool as a launching point to secretly transport the boy to New Zealand, she rushed to the gritty beach town to confront Alf.

John watched as his parents hotly debated their child's future.

"It's your choice," Alf told the five-year-old. "Who do you want to live with?"

"I want you," the confused child answered, still aglow from the holiday they'd been enjoying.

"And you're sure of that?" Julia shouted.

Hesitantly, John nodded.

Pained by the little boy's decision, Julia huffed down the road. Moments later, she heard John sobbing for his mother. She turned to see him rushing up behind her, with his arms spread wide.

Alf left the country. As John told British author Hunter Davies, "It was like he was dead."

■ ■ ■

Mark David Chapman strode up Central Park West toward the Dakota, his mind flashing back to that morning, when he'd stared at his reflection in the hotel mirror, practicing his aim. The next time that he held the gun in his hand, he realized, he wouldn't be play-acting. If he survived the incident, he didn't intend to talk. Instead, the copy of *The Catcher in the Rye* would say it all.

The sights of New York reminded Chapman of that scene in the book when the main character, Holden Caulfield, goes into the city with his school's fencing team, and leaves the foils on the subway. The meet is canceled, and everyone's mad at Houlden. "The whole team ostracized me the whole way back on the train," Houlden tells the reader. "It was pretty funny, in a way."

But Chapman knew it wasn't really funny. He'd been ostracized the same way—ostracized and ignored. And it didn't feel good at all.

■ ■ ■

Alan Weiss's fondness for the Beatles began to wane when the group broke up in 1970. He'd heard the songs from *Double Fantasy* on the radio, and liked them well enough. But, in Weiss' mind, none of the Beatles' solo ventures compared to those of the Fab Four.

Not that he had much time to contemplate these matters. As the senior program producer for WABC News in New York, he had bigger things to worry about than Beatles music. In 1968, news director Al Primo had changed the face of American television news when he imported his "Eyewitness News" concept from Philadelphia. In a prelude to tabloid TV, the broadcast began with a fast-paced melody reminiscent of a teletype machine. The flavor was urban and, primarily, young, and the reporters were depicted less as news readers and more as personalities who related to the tribulations of their interview subjects in Washington Heights and Coney Island. Over the years, alumni would include Tom Snyder, Howard Cosell, Jim Bouton—the former New York Yankee who rattled the baseball world when he authored the insider book *Ball Four*—Rose Ann Scamardella, the inspiration for Gilda Radner's Roseanne Roseannadanna character on *Saturday Night Live*—and John Lennon's friend, Geraldo Rivera.

On December 8, 1980, Weiss was constantly revising the 6:00 P.M. newscast, keeping his eye on stories about graffiti vandals, New York area relatives of the hostages in Tehran, and demonstrators preparing to greet President-elect Reagan around the city. He'd risen to his position earlier in the year, as transportation workers were going on strike. WABC management responded to the crisis by starting the news at 4:30 in the afternoon, in order to inform viewers about the traffic conditions they might encounter. That meant filling the airwaves with ninety minutes of additional airtime, and working out a system to ensure that footage shot in the field appeared on the airwaves in the most efficient manner.

New York was one of the last cities to incorporate satellite trucks into local news operations. As Weiss later explained, when a station in Wichita or Tacoma expanded its coverage, only one or two live trucks were required. "If it doesn't work, it's no big deal. But you get it in New York, you have to buy twenty of each thing. And therefore, you had to make sure everything worked. So you tested it first in smaller markets."

In 1980, some cameramen were still shooting on film. Although live trucks now existed, they were in their infancy in New York, so WABC had to come up with a plan to get their footage back to the studio. Anticipating large traffic jams generated by the strike, the station purchased a number of small motorcycles for its couriers.

"When the strike was over," Weiss said, "the couriers didn't want to use the motorcycles any longer. I guess they were a bit dangerous for New York City." As a result, WABC had put the items up for sale. Weiss purchased one for just under $650.

On this particular day, he was thinking past the evening's broadcast. When the show was over, he had a date on the other side of Manhattan. He'd use his motorcycle, he concluded, to cut across across Central Park. There was no faster way to get around.

■　■　■

At a certain point, because of Julia's unstructured life, the family decided that it would be best for John to move in with her older sister, Mary—known forever to Beatle fans as Aunt Mimi.

Although John obviously preferred his mother—both as a cohort and for the requisite emotional reasons—he knew that the extended family cared about him. Her rules notwithstanding, he liked staying at Mimi's house, particularly because it was located around the corner from a Salvation Army children's home called Strawberry Field. During the summer, Strawberry Field hosted concerts and other community events, and John's friends would frequently call for him first, then walk to the facility. Later, they'd play in the adjoining woods, pluralizing the name of the home to dub the forested area Strawberry Fields.

John told *Playboy* years afterward,

> Strawberry Fields is a real place. After I stopped living at Penny Lane, I moved in with my auntie . . . in a nice, semi-detached place with a small garden, and doctors and lawyers and that ilk around. . . . In the class system, it was about half a class higher than Paul, George and Ringo, who lived in government-subsidized housing. We owned our house and had a garden. . . . Near the home was Strawberry Fields . . . where I used to go to garden parties as a kid. . . . We would go there and hang out, and sell lemonade bottles for a penny. We always had fun at Strawberry Fields. So that's where I got the name. But I used it as an image—Strawberry Fields forever.

Mimi might have been old-fashioned, but she appreciated John's natural talents, so long as they were directed toward something that might advance him in society. With her support, John joined the choir at St. Peter's Church. He apparently liked singing in front of an audience, but quickly began to undermine himself. When the church held a harvest festival, John and his friends noticed batches of grapes hung among the decorations. They swiped and ate the fruit, not necessarily because they liked the taste of grapes but because it was something that they'd been warned *not* to do. Because of this, John and the other boys were banned from the choir.

Mimi was angry and concerned. It wasn't the deed of snatching the grapes that troubled her. The bigger worry was whether the disobedience the boy had learned from his parents might prevent him from breaking free of their less than exalted destiny.

Mimi's husband, George, tried forming a camaraderie with John, reading with him and taking the boy out for the day on long walks. Uncle George was different from Mimi—he gambled and had noticeable flaws—and John grew very fond of him. George was equally attached to his nephew, purchasing him a bike and harmonica. A grateful John kept the instrument in his pocket, impressing friends by playing it on the bus. "I also had a little accordion," John told the *Record Mirror*, a pop music tabloid, in 1971. "I used to play only the right hand, and I played the same things I played on the mouth organ."

Among the ten-year-old's favorites: "Moulin Rouge," "Swedish Rhadsody," and "Greensleeves."

"I always wondered, 'Why hasn't anybody discovered me?'" he told *Rolling Stone* publisher Jann Wenner in a 1970 interview. "Didn't they see that I'm cleverer than anybody in this school, that the teachers are stupid, too?"

To a degree, Aunt Mimi and Uncle George believed that John *was* endowed with special talents, and that those gifts could be channeled in a socially productive manner. Julia was an anomaly, but the rest of the Stanleys were fruitful, upright citizens, they reasoned. The challenge was teaching John to be less like a Lennon, and more like a Stanley. Then, in 1955, fifty-two-year-old George dropped dead from a sudden hemorrhage.

More than ever, John was convinced that anything that appeared to be good would eventually turn bad.

Even Bobby Dykins, the handsome wine steward who moved in with Julia after all her upheavals, had a dark side, beating John's mother after drinking too much. Nonetheless, as John grew into his teens, he frequently stayed overnight at his mother's house, teasing his half-sisters, Julia and Jackie, by holding their school-work above his head where they couldn't reach it. John and the girls loved how their mother played the accordion while singing children's songs. When she came to a particularly dramatic point—the main character spying on the Teddy bears having their picnic, for instance—her fingers moved quickly, and the sound would take a dreamy turn, not unlike the calliope in the Beatles tune "Being for the Benefit of Mr. Kite."

After Paul joined John's band, he became a regular in the house as well, rehearsing in the bathroom, where McCartney claimed the acoustics were akin to a recording studio. At Quarrymen shows, Julia would plant herself in the crowd, dancing to the music, and whistling and clapping louder than anyone else. "We were so happy," John's sister Julia Baird wrote in her book, *Imagine This*. "I was living happiness, and I didn't know it wasn't going to get any better than that."

As soon as John's mother died, Dykins whisked his daughters away to Scotland, too broken to tell the girls about the accident. John remained behind, refusing to view his mother's corpse at Sefton General Hospital, and placing his head on Aunt Mimi's lap at the funeral. In the months that followed, he refused to talk to Nigel Whalley, the friend who'd last seen Julia alive, associating the boy with the tragedy.

Eric Clague, the man whose car struck Julia, considered contacting the family to offer his condolences, but feared an angry backlash. When an inquest was held about the episode, a furious Mimi pointed at the constable and screamed, "Murderer!"

A coroner stated that Julia appeared to have stepped off the curb without watching where she was going. Like her son, her mind was on issues far less banal than the proper way to cross the street.

John's natural mistrust of the institutions that were supposed to protect him evolved into rank hatred. It was a wariness he'd only discard when Sean came into his life and the ex-Beatle could look away from the music industry, enjoying mornings in the apartment, afternoons in the park, and the ever-present buoyancy of the city around him.

5

THIN ICE

George Harrison was feeling disenchanted with the business of rock 'n' roll.

It had been more than a year since he'd begun work on his latest album. George wasn't particularly motivated to speed through the process, a stark contrast from the early Beatle days when the group would churn out two or three albums a year. Nor did George feel compelled to release music solely for its commercial potential; just because record executives seemed enamored with New Wave at the time, didn't mean that Harrison had to record it. In September 1980, when he delivered his first version of *Somewhere in England*, Warner Brothers was underwhelmed. His Beatle past notwithstanding, four of the cuts were rejected outright. "Too dismal," he was told. "Too downbeat."

What did a bunch of suits know, anyway? They even hated the cover art. Disgruntled, Harrison had just returned to the studio, Friar Park in Henley-on-Thames, in November to come up with replacements. He was heartened to be joined by Ringo. In addition to working on George's album, the pair recorded a cover version of "You Belong to Me" for Ringo's next release, *Stop and Smell the Roses*.

George was always happy to help Ringo. It seemed like everyone was. Ringo might have had his drinking issues, but he was a genuinely decent bloke, and everybody liked him. The same couldn't be said for John Lennon. There was always drama with John. The latest was his reaction to George's book, *I Me Mine*. According to John, George had praised virtually every musician with whom he'd worked, except him. George was just exasperated by the whole thing. What about all those years when John and Paul had completely overshadowed him? Did they have any misgivings over that? Despite having been elevated to godly status by just about everyone else in the world, John sent out word that he'd been hurt by *I Me Mine*.

A more insecure man there'd never been.

What did Lennon want? When people told the Beatles story, they always identified the magic moment as the fateful meeting between John Lennon and Paul McCartney. What seemed lost to the so-called historians was George Harrison's role. He'd had his own guitar since age thirteen, and had become friends with McCartney even before John entered the picture. After the Quarrymen were formed, Paul recognized that the younger boy was a prodigious musician and asked him to audition for John in the back of a bus. George was just a year younger than Paul and two years younger than John, but Lennon complained that Paul was forcing a "bloody kid" on him. Then he heard George play, and the mood quickly shifted.

Remarkably, George dropped out of the band at one point to become an apprentice electrician. But the vocation didn't suit him, and he was soon back in the group. Both musically and philosophically, George may have had the greatest influence on the Beatles. But Paul always referred to him as a "baby brother."

Paul thought that he was speaking with affection. But George felt belittled and patronized. In his mind, neither Paul nor John could ever break out of their teenage mindset and see him as an equal member.

■ ■ ■

In Manhattan, John was getting his hair cut. It was late morning, and he and Yoko were in promotion mode now, trying to sell their record. So far, it had gone well. So many of the other hits on the radio—Captain & Tennille's "Do That to Me One More Time,"

Blondie's "Call Me," Queen's "Crazy Little Thing Called Love"—kept the listener bogged down in the seventies, while *Double Fantasy* was a jolt, a journey into the next decade. Not only did people appreciate the music, but John felt that he—not some record company or public relations firm—was controlling the process. He had to thank Yoko for that, too. The public never understood the degree of her business acumen, but it clearly played a role in *Double Fantasy's* success.

When John returned to the Dakota, he and Yoko had a photo shoot scheduled with their upstairs neighbor, Annie Leibovitz, followed by a radio interview. Then the pair would go over to the studio and put the finishing journey on "Walking on Thin Ice."

From a rock star's perspective, John couldn't have been having a better day.

In 1970, three years after Jann Wenner founded *Rolling Stone*, then in San Francisco, Leibovitz—a former painting student at the San Francisco Art Institute—showed him her portfolio. Wenner liked it, and gave Annie her first assignment for the publication. The end result: a black-and-white cover photo of a tousle-haired John Lennon in denim shirt and overalls, his eyes intense behind thick glasses. There were none of the goofy mannerisms he and his bandmates had exhibited in the Beatles. John's mouth was a slightly crooked line framed by a neatly trimmed beard. The photo said a lot about Lennon's perception of himself as a musician: the post-adolescence that was the Beatles was officially over. John was an adult, and his own man.

John had been on magazine covers all over the world. But this particular image meant something to him. It was as much a statement about his frame of mind at this critical stage of his career as it was about the talents of the photographer.

The exposure in *Rolling Stone* engrained Leibovitz into the rock world. In 1975, the Rolling Stones chose her as official photographer for their world tour. Annie took hundreds of photos. Perhaps the best-remembered one was a black-and-white posed shot of Mick

Jagger and Keith Richards. Both were shirtless, but Keith was vamping it up in a bandanna and a white scarf, his stomach thrust toward the camera. By contrast, Mick looked shyly into the lens, his demeanor reflecting more a schoolboy posing for a team photo in a yearbook than a rock star.

Once again, Leibovitz had created another iconic *Rolling Stone* cover.

The Lennons considered Annie their friend. Annie liked them, too, but she didn't take the relationship casually. "They seemed like gods to me," she told *Rolling Stone*. "I remember being impressed with the simple kiss they did on the cover of *Double Fantasy*. The eighties were not a romantic era, and the kiss was just so beautiful."

Annie did not know that John had gotten his hair trimmed until she entered the Lennons' apartment. If he'd asked her about it ahead of time, she probably would have disapproved. The photo session on December 8 had started five days earlier, and now John looked different. Although Annie wasn't exactly mad, she did wonder what had possessed him to change his appearance.

John explained that he'd had long hair since he was a Beatle. He liked the look, he pointed out, "but it takes a lot of keeping up."

The matter was quickly dropped. A more important concern was the type of image John would present to the world. Leibovitz had promised the ex-Beatle another *Rolling Stone* cover, and tried to maneuver him somewhere for a nice solo shot. Yoko and John made eye contact. This wasn't what they wanted. John and Yoko had made *Double Fantasy* as a team, and that's how they wished to be depicted. Annie felt torn. The editors at *Rolling Stone* were interested in a cover featuring John—John Lennon without his wife. But this was a battle that John and Yoko had been fighting since she first began attending Beatles rehearsals. And they knew how to win.

If you wanted John, you got John and Yoko. Take it or leave it.

The Lennons knew that Annie wasn't the problem. It was those thickheads—as Julia Lennon would have said—sitting in a conference room somewhere. Annie was pleased to enjoy their trust, and wasn't about to do anything to weaken it. She looked around the room. It was sunny, and overlooked the park. John and Yoko were happy. So Leibovitz asked them to take off their clothes and embrace.

John immediately disrobed. But for some reason, Yoko demurred. The couple had posed nude numerous times in the past, and she'd never seemed inhibited. Why did she suddenly feel anxious now? Annie respected the Lennons too much to do anything to add to the discomfort. She just hung back, allowing Yoko to take the next step.

"I'll take the shirt off, but not the pants," Yoko offered.

Annie was disappointed, but adaptable. "Just leave everything on," she said.

Relaxed, Yoko lay down and closed her eyes. A nude John curled up beside her, bending a leg and draping it over her torso. He, too, closed his eyes, and kissed the side of her face. "You couldn't help but feel that she was cold, and it looked like he was clinging to her," Leibovitz would recount.

She took a Polaroid, and knew that this was a very special moment. After all the wounds of his childhood, John, nude and vulnerable, felt safest when he hugged the mighty woman he called "Mother." *An all-time ugly photo*

■　■　■

Chapman squinted. The walk toward the Dakota was a sensory assault: blurs of yellow taxis and people running in between moving cars, pretty girls smoking against the long stone wall lining Central Park West, pieces of leaves and bits of newspaper and candy wrappers swirling in the wind, the sound and smell of vendors placing salty pretzels on charcoal. Suddenly, he realized that he was missing something. He always carried *The Catcher in the Rye* with him; now it had been left behind. He couldn't continue to the Dakota without it. At the next light, Chapman joined a crowd in the crosswalk and moved toward Broadway. Then he popped into a bookstore to buy another copy of *The Catcher in the Rye.*

Holden Caulfield wasn't violent, Chapman thought, even if he did engage in a fantasy of emptying a revolver into someone's stomach, a phony who'd betrayed him. The visitor tried to find some justification for what he was about to do. The world needed him, he was convinced, and the act would turn him into a real-life Holden Caulfield, a "quasi-savior," a "guardian angel."

His name would be spoken in the same breath as John, Paul, George, and Ringo.

■   ■   ■

Realizing that John was never going to be a businessman or work on the docks, Aunt Mimi encouraged her nephew to attend Liverpool College of Art, even accompanying him on the entrance interview. For the first time, John was in an environment where the majority of his peers understood him. In figure drawing class, students tried overlooking the fact that a nude woman was standing in front of them. But John—who'd always felt awkward to begin with—drew attention to the collective sense of unease, letting out a loud shriek, waiting a few moments, then following up with a piercing giggle. Soon, the model and pupils were all doubling over in laughter.

Even in the company of fellow artists, John tended to see what others did not. On one occasion, while the other students were concentrating on the contours of the model's body, John sketched the only item that she was wearing, her wristwatch.

Despite its provincial location, Liverpool had a bohemian, scene and finally John was part of it, attending art exhibitions and poetry readings as well as jazz concerts in dark, intimate settings like the Cavern Club.

Coincidentally, George Harrison and Paul McCartney were students at the Liverpool Institute next door, and the two boys would walk over to the art college at lunch, rehearsing with John in a spare room or entertaining the students in a public area with songs by Buddy Holly and the Everly Brothers.

But John's feelings about George were mixed. When Harrison had a guitar in his hands, Lennon was proud to be around him. Otherwise, the younger boy seemed like a pest. "There is a vast difference between being in high school and being in college," John told *Playboy*, "and I was already in college, and already had sexual relationships, already drank, and did a lot of things like that." John never claimed to be mature, but there was something about George that was not fully formed. "We'd come out of art school," John continued, "and he'd be hovering around like those kids at the gate of the Dakota now."

Thelma Pickles was John's first girlfriend at the college. At the time, two-parent families were not just the norm, but the rule—and Thelma's father had left when she was ten. The experience set her apart from her friends, and she'd been too embarrassed to discuss her circumstances until John told her his. "When we were alone together, he was really soft, thoughtful and generous-spirited," she told the *Observer* newspaper. "Clearly, his mother's death had disturbed him. We both felt that we'd been dealt a raw deal."

But the turmoil had had a far uglier effect on John, and his relationship with Thelma fell apart because of it. After an art school dance one night, the two sneaked into a darkened classroom. Thelma anticipated an intimate exchange, but soon realized that other students were also present. The mood wasn't right, and she started to leave the room. Roughly, John pulled her back, then smacked her. "He had aggressive traits, mainly verbal," she recalled. "Once he hit me, that was it for me."

As he would with Yoko later on, John found someone else to make a focal point in his life. Stu Sutcliffe was a handsome, artistic Scotsman partial to dark, mysterious shades and a pompadour that rose slightly higher than the American versions. He and a group of friends were crashing in a derelict Georgian home near the college, and invited John to move in. Always in search of an anchor, John became very attached to Stu, even persuading him to sell one of his paintings and use the funds to buy a bass guitar. Stu couldn't play, but John was sure that would come in time. Either way, John informed his bandmates that Stu was now a member of the group.

Paul was shocked at Stu's lack of musical ability. Both McCartney and Lennon relentlessly teased Sutcliffe about his playing. But he was never asked to leave the group. Stu's presence created too much of a comfort for Lennon, and John was essentially the leader of the band.

John also found a new girlfriend, Cynthia Powell, a shy, attractive girl he'd met in lettering class. Just as Thelma and John bonded over the losses of their respective parents, Cynthia and the future Beatle connected because of their poor vision—a revelation made one afternoon when students were trying on one another's glasses.

"This earth-shattering discovery brought us to a new high point of communication," she'd joke to British writer Kate Shelley in 1980.

At first, Cynthia kept her distance from John. He was such a bombastic force at the college, and one never knew when his humor would turn to ridicule. "He was such a very complex character, even at that age," she told British radio personality Alex Belfield, "because he had such a disjointed and fractured childhood." When he asked her out, she hesitated, noting that she was engaged to a fellow in Hoylake, the orderly suburb where her family lived on the opposite side of the River Mersey.

"I didn't ask you to marry me, did I?" John shouted, characteristically blending his charm with intimidation.

Soon, Cynthia discarded her fiancé and began altering herself to accommodate Lennon, all but apologizing for her "posh" accent and dying her hair to resemble John's favorite actress, Brigitte Bardot.

■ ■ ■

Mark David Chapman may not have realized was that there was already a Chapman interwoven into Beatles history. For a brief period in 1960, Norman Chapman had played with the group—George Harrison considered him the best drummer the Beatles ever had—before joining the military and handing his position off to Pete Best.

John had quit art college by the point, despite Aunt Mimi's protestations. She understood his artistic nature, but thought that a career in art, maybe commercial art, was preferable to guitar. He was such a good illustrator, she argued, why couldn't he just get his degree?

Said John, "I don't need the bits of paper to tell me where I'm going."

For the short term, at least, he was going to the nation then called West Germany.

On August 17, 1960, the band—now officially known as the Beatles—premiered at the Indra Club on the Reeperbahn, the main street in Hamburg's red-light district. Pete played drums behind John, Paul, and George's guitars and Stu Sutcliffe on bass. The group's tour would be a grueling affair, with the band required to play for hours at a time. To maintain their energy, they began ingesting amphetamines.

With teeth chattering and eyes bulging, Lennon became more outrageous than usual, once appearing on stage in an old-fashioned swimsuit with a toilet seat around his neck. But the *frauleins* loved the Beatles, and the squeals of their newfound groupies filled the boys' dilapidated living quarters. Lennon later told interviewer Tom Snyder that the young women they met pursued anyone who performed on stage: "They didn't care if it was a comedian or a man who ate glass."

For the Beatles, Hamburg was a type of boot camp, and the recruits came out the other end as accomplished musicians—entertainers who understood how to channel their collective charisma—in a tight band. Two days after Christmas in 1960, the Beatles showcased their progress at the Town Hall Ballroom in Liverpool. For the first time, the crowd rushed the stage. On a very local level, Beatlemania had begun.

For the next two years, the Beatles would shuttle between Hamburg and Liverpool, developing a fan base in each location. The fame, unfortunately, was accompanied by jealousy; many young men started to hate the Beatles for the sexual energy they radiated toward the local females. On January 30, 1961, Sutcliffe suffered a fractured skull after being severely beaten by a gang as the band loaded their gear after a show at Lathom Hall in Liverpool.

Sutcliffe eventually splintered off from the band—after falling in love in Hamburg with an artist and photographer named Astrid Kirchherr, whose views on fashion and culture would greatly influence the group. John called Astrid and her friends "Exys," his personal term for existentialists. "Our philosophy then, because we were only kids, was wearing black clothes and going around looking moody," she told BBC Radio in 1995. "Of course, we had a clue who Jean Paul Sartre was. We got inspired by all the French artists and writers...and we tried to dress like French existentialists."

Astrid's black-and-white photos of the Beatles' Hamburg period are now considered vital historical items. But, more significantly, she's credited with having changed the Beatles' fundamental look when she asked Stu to "take the Brylcreem out of his hair." The mop top was a popular style among German art students, and Astrid molded her boyfriend's hair the same way. Soon George also altered his hairstyle. Paul and John would follow later, allowing one of Astrid's friends to cut their hair during a trip to Paris. Only Pete Best maintained his pompadour because, in Astrid's words, he had "really curly hair and it wouldn't work."

When Stu and Astrid moved in together, he frequently borrowed her clothes, including a collarless jacket that he wore on stage. John was unimpressed with the fashion, asking his friend, "Did your mother lend you her suit?"

After Stu finally left the Beatles to live with Astrid in Germany, Paul was forced to take over on bass, a chore he initially resented. However, according to Stu's sister, Pauline, it was John who was truly begrudging. In a drunken fit, Pauline told author Larry Kane, John beat his friend bloody, and kicked him in the head: "A writer once challenged me on whether John would beat up Stuart because he loved him so much, and I suggested to the writer that he didn't understand love and that you can love someone and still beat them up."

In fact, Pauline believed that the beating occurred because John was convinced that Stu—like the others before—was leaving him behind.

John and Stu remained friends, and Lennon was looking forward to seeing Sutcliffe when the Beatles returned to Hamburg in April 13, 1962. But when John alighted from the aircraft, Astrid was waiting with heartbreaking news. For months, Stu had been complaining of crippling headaches. Three days earlier, he'd collapsed during an art class, and died in Astrid's arms in the ambulance on the way to the hospital. The official cause of death: cerebral paralysis, due to bleeding in the right ventricle of the brain.

To this day, no one is certain if the brain hemorrhage occurred because of a congenital condition or as a result of the beating outside Lathom Hall. Regardless, John never forgot his friend or the loss. At the Dakota, Stu's name would come up on the average of once a week, with John reminiscing about the friendship to Yoko and claiming to feel his friend's spirit. When *Sgt. Pepper's Lonely Hearts Club Band* was released in 1967, Stu's face was included within the menagerie of faces on the cover—at Lennon's insistence.

With this one act, Stu was again beside the Beatles in a musical setting. Sadly, this couldn't diminish John's pervasive sense of dread about when the next person he loved would unexpectedly depart.

"I've had a lot of people die on me," he told Jann Wenner.

6

"I'm Only a Fan, John"

There'd always been a haunted feel to the Dakota.

Even before the release of *Rosemary's Baby*, the stories of ghosts in the building were urban legends. In the 1960s, painters working in the apartment of recently-deceased actress Judy Holliday claimed to see an apparition of a boy in a Buster Brown suit—with the body of a man and face of a child. On another occasion, a group of workmen reported a sighting of a pallid girl with long, blonde hair and a dress from another era bouncing a ball in the hallway. John's neighbors spoke of hearing footsteps on empty floors and seeing furniture move. And then there were the gargoyles. Depending on the source, the creatures adorning the railing outside the building either worked in concert with the phantoms inside, or warded them off.

Mark David Chapman studied the classical figures as he waited in the cold. There was something distinctly pagan about their appearance, but Chapman didn't feel that his Christian beliefs were being challenged. After contemplating the *porche cochère*, or coach gate, outside the building—built large enough so horse-drawn carriages could fit through the passage and drop off their affluent passengers in an area sheltered from the elements—Chapman opened *The Catcher in the Rye* and started to read.

"I hope to hell when I *do* die, somebody has sense enough to dump me in the river or something." It didn't matter how many times he examined the book—Holden Caulfield always seemed to speak directly to him. But on this occasion, he was so absorbed in the book that he felt completely detached from the bustle of activity around him. And later, he'd wonder whether he'd missed John Lennon darting out the front of the Dakota into a taxi.

At 12:30 P.M., there were only two other people outside the Dakota, a female fan and Paul Goresh, a twenty-one-year-old amateur photographer from North Arlington, New Jersey. Goresh had become smitten with the Beatles at age seven, when he first heard *Rubber Soul,* and initially entered John Lennon's territory as an invader, getting past security at the Dakota by claiming to be a VCR repairman.

Goresh was shocked when Lennon himself answered the door. The ex-Beatle seemed bewildered that no one had informed him about this visit—particularly because his VCR wasn't broken. Still in character as a technician, Goresh produced a camera, but John told his admirer that he didn't want any pictures in the press; he'd been avoiding the media to raise a family. Nonetheless, Lennon agreed to sign an autograph. Goresh was happy to have proof of some contact with his idol, and decided to wait and photograph Lennon at a later time, outside the Dakota.

A few days later, John noticed Goresh on the block with his photo gear, and became aggravated. This was no VCR repairman! This was a guy who'd sneaked into John's home. The whole concept was outrageous and terrifying, and John rushed up to Goresh and attempted to snatch his camera.

Goresh pushed Lennon away. "Don't do that. You're going to break it."

Lennon wasn't in the mood to be respectful to someone who'd hustled his way into the building—into the same apartment where Sean played and slept—under false pretenses. "I don't want any pictures," he told Goresh.

Goresh realized that John thought that he was a paparazzo. This wasn't the exchange he'd wanted to have with his idol. "I'm only a fan, John," he insisted.

If Paul was only a fan, John reasoned, he could afford to leave the Dakota without his film. "Give me the film," Lennon demanded.

Rewinding the roll in the camera, Goresh handed the film to John. "Could I ask you a favor?" Paul pleaded. "I have two shots that I took. Could you please develop them, and give me the photos for my private collection?"

John refused to contemplate the suggestion. "I told you no pictures," he insisted, exposing the film, then stomping away.

The altercation did nothing to extinguish Goresh's passion. He continued hanging around outside the Dakota, and at some point Lennon realized that this was just a kid who liked the Beatles. The fans who watched for him might have been overzealous, but the former Beatle didn't consider them dangerous. If John was going to live like a New Yorker—listening to the melodic mix of Spanish, Cantonese, and Haitian Creole as he walked up Seventy-second Street—he wanted to get along with the people he saw each day in his neighborhood. So he asked Paul to take a walk with him. John explained that Goresh had scared him, by entering his home with the repairman ruse, and how important it was to value privacy. Goresh apologized.

"As long as you don't have a camera," John said, "we won't have any problems."

Over the next few months, John frequently waved at Goresh outside the building and invited him on strolls. On Columbus Avenue, John would grow exasperated when his fan asked too many questions about the Beatles, and managed to take the conversation in other directions.

"Why don't you tell me a little bit more about you?"

Everybody liked to talk about themselves, especially Beatles fans being encouraged to describe the minutiae of their lives to John Lennon.

Eventually John waived his no-camera restriction and began to treat Goresh as a friend—he remembered what it was like to be a rock 'n' roll fan himself. When cover art was needed for *Watching the Wheels*, the first *Double Fantasy* single, Lennon even picked one of Goresh's photos—of John and Yoko walking past the front gate of the Dakota on a summer day.

A line had been crossed. The fan had become legit.

Chapman could tell that Goresh enjoyed a special position outside the Dakota. He was clearly in with Lennon; workers and even residents of the building went out of their way to greet him. Hoping to ingratiate himself somehow, Chapman walked over to the photographer and shook his hand.

"I'm Mark."

"Hey, Mark. You from around here?"

"Oh, no. Hawaii."

"Hawaii? But it sounds like you have a southern accent."

Chapman nodded, and clarified that he'd been raised in Georgia.

"Is John your favorite musician?"

Chapman shook his head from side to side. "I like John's music. But my all-time favorite is Todd Rundgren."

Since the day seemed uneventful, Goresh continued the small talk: "Where are you staying while you're in town?"

Out of nowhere, Chapman became paranoid and defensive. Accusingly, he turned on Goresh: "Why do you want to know?"

7

UNREALITY

Ringo Starr had another drink. A warm breeze swept in from the ocean as Ringo stared up at the palm trees, smiling crookedly at his girlfriend. He'd met Barbara Bach, a Queens-bred model now remembered as the sultry Bond Girl in *The Spy Who Loved Me*, ten months earlier, when the two were filming the movie *Caveman*, a comedy about prehistoric misfits. It had been a party of sorts ever since, with the pair consuming bountiful amounts of alcohol in different locations. Today they were lounging in a rented house in the Bahamas.

Ringo had always been the sickliest of the Beatles. He'd fallen into a coma at age six, in the midst of a bout of peritonitis. Six months later, while recuperating, he fell out of a hospital bed, injuring himself so badly that he remained incapacitated for an additional half year. At age thirteen, he was stricken with pleurisy. This time, he was hospitalized for two years. By the time he recovered, he didn't even bother returning to the classroom; he'd missed too much school to ever catch up.

On June 3, 1964, on the eve of a breakneck Beatles tour of Scandinavia, Asia, and Australia, Ringo collapsed from a combination of tonsillitis and pharyngitis. Drummer Jimmy Nicol, who'd recorded a variety of Beatles cover tunes, was quickly hired as a replacement, given a mop top haircut, and told to wear Ringo's clothes. During Ringo's convalescence, McCartney telegraphed his bandmate with a simple message: "Hurry up and get well Ringo. Jimmy is wearing out all your suits." Despite his feeble condition, Ringo heeded the advice, resuming his place after Nicol had played just eight shows and left to, among other ventures, substitute for Dave Clark of the Dave Clark Five, who had fallen ill just before a tour, and to open a button factory in Mexico.

Ringo's health problems resurfaced in 1979, when he was hospitalized in Monte Carlo with intestinal troubles tied to his childhood peritonitis. After several feet of intestine were removed, the drummer felt well enough to attend Eric Clapton's wedding with George and Paul. But the year would bring further troubles. Six months later, a fire destroyed Starr's home in Los Angeles, along with a significant collection of his Beatle memorabilia.

Through it all, his old friends in the Beatles remained available to him. Besides George, Paul was also assisting with Ringo's upcoming album, *Stop and Smell the Roses*. While the other Beatles might have had issues with one another, John, Paul, and George were united in their partiality for Ringo. John, for instance, could be miserly with compliments, but he always told interviewers about his reverence for Ringo's skills—as a drummer, singer, and actor. Lennon maintained that those talents would have been recognized whether or not Ringo had ever joined the Beatles.

John's admiration may have been rooted in the fact that, when the Beatles were starting out, Ringo was already an established figure on the Liverpool music scene. In 1959, he'd joined Rory Storm and the Hurricanes. Storm spoke with a pronounced stutter but was charismatic on stage, where his impediment was undetectable. His band worked the same Liverpool-to-Hamburg circuit as the Beatles, but were lodged in more habitable quarters, and paid better. When Pete Best was indisposed, Ringo occasionally filled in with the Beatles. But he was still Rory's drummer, and John was among those who anticipated that the Hurricanes would be the first Liverpool band to make an international impact.

Rory's birth name was Alan Caldwell, but he believed that the Storm moniker was better suited to show business. Likewise, he encouraged the real-life Richard Starkey to find a more crowd-pleasing stage name. Because of his perpetually bejeweled fingers, Starkey chose "Rings" at first, then concluded that "Ringo" evoked images of a country and western personality. Adopting "Starr" came more naturally, and Ringo's solo section during each Hurricanes concert was christened "Starr Time." John, Paul, and George were often in the audience as Ringo glowed in the spotlight, singing cover versions of songs that would later come to be regarded as his own—notably "Boys," previously popularized by the Shirelles, and rockabilly star Johnny Burnette's "You're Sixteen."

■　■　■

If one looked at Pete Best's background, one would have thought him the least likely member of the Beatles to be pushed aside. He was too indispensable. Pete's father grew up in a family of sports promoters whose holdings once included Liverpool Stadium. His mother founded the Casbah Coffee Club, where the Quarrymen, as well as Pete's original band, the Black Jacks, performed some of their early shows. After Pete joined the Beatles, the group regularly played the Casbah, which boasted membership rolls of more than 1,000.

Then Brian Epstein entered the Beatles' universe, neutralizing the Bests and—either by design or by default—bringing in Ringo.

The Epstein family was in the furniture business, and owned a chain of retail outlets called NEMS, for North End Music Stores. All of the Beatles were customers and had seen Brian, dressed smartly, conferring with clerks and shoppers. As in the Lennon home, there was a strained dynamic in the Epstein household. Brian had been forced to work in the family's businesses, despite the fact that he'd aspired to be a dress designer. Although a prolific salesman, Brian was unhappy. Eventually, Harry Epstein, Brian's father, allowed him to study acting in London, but when the endeavor went nowhere, the young man eventually returned to Liverpool, where he labored tirelessly to build the NEMS franchise.

On November 9, 1961, Epstein stopped by the Cavern Club to catch a lunchtime performance by the Beatles. When he and a colleague entered the backstage area afterwards, he was immediately recognized.

"And what brings Mr. Epstein here?" George Harrison blurted.

"We just popped in to say hello," Brian answered in an educated accent. "I enjoyed your performance."

But the theatrical young man wished to be more than just a fan. Perhaps the Beatles could rescue him from the grasp of his stern Jewish family, and bring him someplace more glamorous. In particular, Epstein was fascinated by John Lennon, the rough boy in the leather pants, who also seemed a little bit different, a little deeper, than his peers. The attraction was not reciprocated. Nonetheless, John sensed that Brian possessed the connections to take the Beatles further than they'd ever been, as well as maybe even an understanding of the loneliness John often felt.

At the time, homosexuality was illegal in England, and when Brian cruised the bars and clubs frequented by others of his persuasion, he felt a mixture of titillation, fear, and self-loathing. Yet he couldn't stay away from the gay districts in the cities he visited, and was periodically picked up by the police. While in the Army, he embarrassed his family with an encounter that led to his discharge on grounds of being "emotionally and mentally unfit."

Perhaps if he managed the Beatles, Brian fantasized, he could attain the respectability that a man of his tastes and work ethic warranted.

Aunt Mimi warned John that Epstein's efforts at managing might be a temporary lark for an indulged son of a wealthy family. When the next fashion came along, she feared, Epstein would drop the group like a forgotten toy. Interestingly, Brian's parents also had reservations. They had an expanding business and didn't need their son distracted by a rock 'n' roll act. To placate them, Epstein promised that the Beatles would simply serve as a pleasurable sideline. His first priority, of course, would be the NEMS outlets.

Only Pete Best's mother encouraged her son to go with Epstein.

As soon as the deal was consummated—on January 24, 1962—Brian began scrutinizing every element of the band's presentation. In Liverpool, fan loyalties tended to be divided between the Everton and Liverpool Football Clubs, so Epstein instructed the lads never to talk about soccer. Furthermore, the Beatles were no longer to behave like a bar band, dressing in jeans and leather jackets, or stopping songs to take requests from a random audience member. From now on, Epstein decreed, the boys would act like they belonged in a concert hall or theater—no more eating or cursing on stage—bowing in synch when the show was over.

But they had to look like the type of people who bowed. So Brian told his charges to start wearing suits and ties at performances. Lennon resisted—he was a rock 'n' roll musician, not an actuary. Paul countered that Epstein's formula could propel the Beatles past the other bands on the scene.

"Yeah, man, all right," John relented. "I'll wear a suit. I'll wear a bloody balloon if somebody's going to pay me."

At the time of the contract, John was twenty-one and Epstein twenty-seven. But Brian seemed infinitely more worldly, and tried projecting his polished demeanor onto the group. "He gave them taste," George Martin told the E! network. "He gave them their charm and their impeccability in dress. He was quite strict in dressing them up. He made them bow....Brian gave them all that....He had a great deal of talent."

It was Epstein who brought the Beatles to Martin, who'd previously produced comedy and novelty records, and recorded regional music around the British Isles. Martin was now affiliated with Parlophone, an imprint of EMI generally given over to marginal acts. The first audition was troublesome, with Pete Best's drumming failing to impress.

There had been other issues with Pete. He was more withdrawn than the other Beatles, and still wore his hair like a Teddy Boy from the 1950s. Plus, according to rumor, there was jealousy, at least on George and Paul's part, over Pete's good looks. So Epstein was assigned the task of firing the drummer and replacing him with Ringo.

Pete was furious. After all, his mother had helped build the band's following at the Casbah. He was particularly hurt by the fact that the normally direct Lennon refused to discuss the matter one on one. John later claimed that he wanted to avoid a fistfight. Still, he admitted that he and his fellow Beatles had acted like "cowards."

For a while, Martin was uncertain about whether Ringo would fit into the group. During one recording session, another drummer was brought in, and an unhappy Ringo was demoted to shaking the maracas and a tambourine. However, when *Love Me Do* was released in the fall of 1962, Ringo was the one playing the drums. By the time it hit #17 on the British charts in December, no one ever contemplated shuffling him out of the band again.

■ ■ ■

Mark Chapman was seven years old at the time, the unhappy son of an Air Force staff sergeant and nurse. Chapman had been born outside Fort Worth, Texas. But after his discharge, Mark's father, David, found a job in the American Oil Company's credit department and relocated the family to the Atlanta suburb of Decatur.

On the surface, the Chapmans appeared to be a basic, upwardly mobile American family. Behind closed doors, though, Chapman described an atmosphere of mistrust, dread, and sudden violence. David allegedly had a quick temper, physically lashing out at both his son and his wife. The incidents would terrify and enrage the younger Chapman when he heard his mother scream out in the middle of the night. At times, Mark claimed, he sat on the floor beside his mother, rubbing her leg in a vain effort to assuage her pain.

Chapman described his father as a man who simply didn't apologize for his actions. David apparently never hugged his son or expressed any type of love. Similarly, Mark felt little affection toward David, visualizing instead a scenario in which he confronted his father with a gun, then shot him dead.

At school, Chapman was anxious and clumsy, a failure at sports and an easy target for boys who detected his weakness. Unable to cope, he'd overreact to the kind of roughhousing and teasing that his peers could tolerate, inviting even more scorn.

It was only when he was alone—away from those who scared and abused him—that Chapman was able to feel a sense of control. In his mind, he created a universe of invisible little people who'd wait for his commands. The little people loved Chapman because he was their king, and they served at his pleasure. At home, reading a book or watching television, he'd peer at the walls and the base-boards, and practically hear the little people scurrying up towards the ceiling. When the little people pleased him, he'd dole out rewards. If they disappointed him, he'd show vengeance, pushing in the button on the sofa and blowing them up.

The little people were Chapman's buffer from the rest of the world—until he discovered the Beatles. While every other reality element stayed outside, Chapman opened the door a crack and allowed the Beatles to enter. He knew all their names and memo-rized all their songs. Lining up his green plastic soldiers on the floor, Chapman drew tiny guitars and pasted it over the rifles. Then he'd play a Beatles record and put on a concert for the little people.

The little people were Beatles fans, too. Only they and Chapman understood that many of the songs had been written for him.

The world loved the Beatles, the same way that the little people loved Chapman. But why couldn't everybody else feel the same way?

They would, Chapman thought, if he became a Beatle himself.

■ ■ ■

One of the reasons John Lennon clung to his small family was that he was grateful for something he'd never expected to attain. Although the Beatles' achievements allowed John to purchase whatever he wished, a stable home seemed perennially evasive. Yet, just as the Beatles were becoming English deities, John thought he had this goal in sight—after his girlfriend, Cynthia Powell, informed him that she was pregnant. Another young man in Lennon's position might have felt trapped. But John appeared to be as excited about the baby as he was by the possibility of ruling the charts. Immediately, he asked Cynthia to marry him.

Cynthia was delighted. Aunt Mimi was not. She feared that the tasks of fatherhood would overwhelm her nephew before his life really started. While John gave little thought to the tedious mission of raising a child, he embraced the idea of bringing up a baby whose father would never disappear.

Neither John nor Cynthia realized that, even at this early juncture, they'd never have independence from the Beatles. Nonetheless, John was already strategizing about his position in the group, choosing the influential Brian Epstein as his best man.

The young couple married quickly, in an austere civil ceremony. With construction under way behind the registrar's building, the sound of a pneumatic drill drowned out much of the procedure. It was such a confusing scene that when the groom was asked to come forward, George Harrison stepped away from Paul McCartney to stand beside Cynthia. Epstein—whose homosexuality set him apart from his relatives and social peers—seemed genuinely touched that John had placed such high value on their friendship and, afterwards, hosted a small reception at Reece's in Clayton Square—the very same location where Alf and Julia Lennon had celebrated their union. Then the Beatles rushed to the Riverpark Ballroom in Chester to perform a gig.

While Cynthia was pregnant, Epstein allowed the Lennons to live in his apartment, then paid for a private room at Sefton General Hospital for the birth. On April 8, 1963, John Charles Julian Lennon was born. Putting business first, John was on tour that day—and kept a promise to Epstein by making him the boy's godfather.

By this time, Beatlemania had struck in Great Britian. The group's second single, "Please Please Me," had rocketed to #2 in February, and an album of thirteen songs—including "Misery," "Twist and Shout," and "Do You Want to Know a Secret?"—was quickly churned out. Cynthia and the baby were not to partake in the excitement. The image-conscious Epstein wanted fans to believe that every member of the Beatles was single—and available.

Cynthia and Julian hid out in a downstairs apartment at Aunt Mimi's house, their existence kept secret not only from the public, but even from Ringo, who, as the newest member of the Beatles, wasn't yet privy to such classified data.

"I felt as if I was never there," Cynthia told writer Kate Shelley. "I walked through a decade like a ghost. In the end, the Beatles were all married to each other."

Even John conceded that "unreality" became his reality.

Despite his pledge to provide a grounded life for his child, John didn't even see Julian until the boy was three days old. At the end of a series of concerts, John blew into Liverpool and was introduced to his son, then almost immediately left town again. Oddly, the Beatles did not have any concerts booked for the next several days. But John told Cynthia that he was accompanying Brian on a vacation to Spain. He explained that it was important to ingratiate himself with the manager because, long after the Beatles ceased to exist, Brian would be involved in some other lucrative deal, and John hoped to ride along with him. (Some also believe that John wanted to use this vacation to establish with Epstein that there was one leader of the Beatles, and it wasn't Paul.)

John had also grown fond of the manager for, among other things, opening up a curtain to worlds the provincial band members never could have discovered on their own. Although heterosexual, John was curious about a lifestyle that was apparently so threatening to society that it was banned. In Spain, he'd sit with Brian in Torremolinos and watch other gay men parade by. Curious about how Brian thought, the Beatle would inquire about which males his manager found attractive, and why. John later said that he felt like an investigative journalist. ○ ⦗

According to John, the relationship was strictly platonic. But longtime Lennon friend Pete Shotton would later contend that a drunken John allowed Brian to masturbate him, essentially to learn what a homosexual encounter was like.

Needless to say, the nature of the friendship was a major topic of discussion in Liverpool music circles. Brian's predisposition was obvious the moment one met him. But John? When Bob Wooler, the Cavern Club disc jockey who'd introduced the Beatles on stage, decided to tease John about this at Paul's twenty-first birthday party, an inebriated Lennon slugged him. A photo of the altercation was featured on the back page of the *Daily Mirror*, but the press did not wish to pursue the matter further. As Epstein told his reporter friends in private, the Beatles were only going to get bigger, and no one wanted to be banished.

Unfortunately for Cynthia, she already was. Even when the media finally acknowledged John's domestic circumstances, Cynthia was treated as an outsider whose role it was to quietly raise John's child without interfering with the escalation of his superstardom. On those sporadic occasions when John happened to be in the house, she was expected to dutifully bring him his newspapers and breakfast in bed, usually after he'd woken up, sometime in the afternoon.

"Being with a famous man isn't all it's cracked up to be," she told Kate Shelley. "In fact, it gets very boring. They're not interested in you, not really. They're totally surrounded by their own aura, fascinated with themselves."

Years later, John realized how'd he'd taken Cynthia for granted, even writing a song about females in her position called "Woman is the Nigger of the World": "We tell her home is the only place she should be / Then we complain that she's too unworldly."

Of course, John never expressed this type of remorse during his marriage to Cynthia; he was too busy being a Beatle. It was only after he fell in love with his second wife that he grasped the extent of the sorrow he'd caused the first.

■ ■ ■

The more famous the Beatles became, the more John tended to doubt himself. Sooner or later, he worried, his fans were going to figure out that he was a terrible singer. Occasionally, John asked George Martin to downplay his voice while mixing a song. In Lennon's own estimation, he sounded screechy. Clearly, the record-buying public didn't think so. As for Martin, he was thrilled to have a group that could literally grind out a hit in a single take.

The Beatles had yet to cross the Atlantic when, in January 1964, "I Want to Hold Your Hand" became the #1 song on the American charts. On February 7, 1964, when the Beatles landed at New York's John F. Kennedy Airport for the start of their first U.S. tour, John showcased his impish cynicism to this new market.

"Why does your music excite people so much?" he was asked at a press conference, with the screams of 3,000 fans echoing through the airport's corridors.

"If we knew, we'd form another group and be managers."

John was questioned about whether his parents had been in show business.

"No," he countered, working in some risqué double entendre, "but I'm told my dad was a great performer."

The assembled reporters laughed out loud. This guy could turn a phrase better than them! The next day's stories were valentines to the Beatles. But the group was just getting started. Two nights later, the band appeared on *The Ed Sullivan Show*. Fifty thousand requests had come in for the studio's 703 seats. The greatest American TV audience ever assembled—an incredible seventy-three million people—watched the broadcast. Just about everybody described the moment as a watershed event. This was more than Beatlemania. The song set—"All My Loving," "Till There Was You,"

"She Loves You," "I Saw Her Standing There," and "I Want to Hold Your Hand"—transformed people forever.

While the girls swooned, the authoritative Sullivan endorsed the Beatles' character to wary parents, calling the lads "four of the nicest youngsters we've ever had on our stage." The sixty-two-year-old host television host declared himself one of the group's "most rabid fans."

Interestingly, the American marketing strategy involved depicting Lennon as a good family man. When the cameras focused on him during the rendition of "Till There Was You"—a song written for the play *The Music Man*, and performed by future gay rights adversary Anita Bryant in 1959—a graphic proclaimed, "Sorry Girls, He's Married."

Soon, American stores were flooded with Beatles watches, drinking mugs and bubblegum cards. One company manufactured 15,000 Beatle wigs a day. Even Brian Epstein enhanced his standing with a gig as a special British correspondent for the American music show *Hullabaloo*. By early 1965, the Beatles were the top recording act of any kind in the United States.

Said Sid Bernstein, the impresario responsible for promoting what was then the biggest rock concert in history, at New York's Shea Stadium, "Only Hitler ever duplicated their power over crowds." *Hitler was long dead.*
They duplicated his power

■ ■ ■

Apparently, the British royal family concurred with this assessment. On October 26, 1965, Queen Elizabeth II herself made all four Beatles Members of the Most Excellent Order of the British Empire (MBE). George joked that the letters actually stood for "Mr. Brian Epstein." But John had real misgivings about accepting the honor. He was distrustful of the royals and Britain's imperialist adventures. And he was deeply uncomfortable with the idea of being elevated above the rest of society. The pop star being extolled, he maintained, bore no resemblance to John Lennon, the kid from the broken family who had to be raised by his Aunt Mimi. Two years earlier, before playing *Twist and Shout* for the queen, queen mother, and Princess Margaret, John subtly showed his disdain for his country's ruling class when he said, "For our last number, I'd like to ask your help. The people in the cheaper seats, clap your hands. And the rest of you, just rattle your jewelry."

He later claimed that he'd intended to say "fuckin' jewelry," but was talked out of sabotaging the group's upward mobility by McCartney and Epstein.

Everybody seemed to like the Beatles, even those who should have dismissed the Fab Four as bubblegum rockers. Bob Dylan recalled driving through Colorado with his band, and noticing that the Beatles commanded eight spots on the Top 10. Rather than deprecating Beatlemania as a trivial fad, Dylan heard chords and harmonies that opened his thoughts. "They were doing things nobody was doing," he told biographer Anthony Scaduto. "I knew they were pointing the direction of where music had to go."

With advocates as diverse as Dylan and the queen, the Beatles were making more money than the members could ever spend. John purchased a four-bedroom house for his half-sisters, Jackie and Julia. At Lennon's own home, sacks of fan mail were delivered every day. McCartney received a comparable amount, but with an unusual twist. The man who transported the parcels was Eric Clague, the former constable who had run over Julia Lennon and left the police force to work for the postal service.

The chance assignment wasn't pleasant for Paul or for Clague. "I used to deliver hundreds of cards and letters to the house," the postman later told the *Sunday Mirror*. "I remember struggling up the path with them all. But, of course, they just reminded me of John Lennon and his mother."

The coincidence freaked Lennon out, and fueled the paranoia all the Beatles felt in the wake of sudden fame. During one North American trip, George refused to appear in a San Francisco parade, fearing the fate suffered by John F. Kennedy riding in that motorcade through Dallas. At a Montreal show, Ringo positioned his cymbals high, just in case an assassin was lurking in the balcony. John, whose life experiences had engendered an unnatural fixation with death, began theorizing about the conditions of his demise: "We'll either go in a plane or we'll be popped off by some loony."

8

"And Now, It's All This"

In the ninth grade, Mark David Chapman grew his hair long and began dressing like John Lennon. When the topic of the Beatles came up, he'd overlook Paul, George, and Ringo to focus on his idol. Nothing Lennon could do was wrong; Chapman even laughed at the Beatle's statements questioning the validity of Christianity. Mark smoked pot, dropped acid, and claimed to have tried heroin. While tripping one day, he realized that he was capable of murder, gazing at a knife and contemplating the act of randomly thrusting it into one of his friends. At that point of his life, though, the mechanisms were in place to prevent Mark from following through on his fantasy.

When not drugging with his acquaintances, Chapman was left with his gnawing self-doubts. He skipped classes because he didn't see the point of getting an education. Not him. He was "useless" and "a nobody."

His first encounter with law enforcement occurred when he was fourteen and acting irrational on acid. Cops picked him up and charged him with vagrancy. After a night in jail, Mark was released into his parents' custody. His mother was so upset about his new habits and associations that she locked him in his room. When she went into another part of the house, he unhinged the door and ran off for a week, staying with a friend. Even after he returned, he felt strangled by Decatur and took off to Miami. This was his chance to break away and live on his own terms—rejecting his parents' rules and recreating himself in the image of a Beatles song. For two weeks, he hung out on the streets and on the beach.

But he didn't have the heart to stay there. With each passing day, he became homesick for the familiar misery at home—until a man he'd met purchased him a bus ticket back to Georgia.

■   ■   ■

For a group of guys raised in a country where homosexuality was forbidden, the Beatles were extremely understanding of Brian Epstein's lifestyle. Paul explained that Epstein's network of gay friends helped expand the Beatles artistically. It was Epstein who connected the Beatles with Robert Fraser. As a British officer in Africa in the 1950s, Fraser was rumored to have had a sexual relationship with a youthful Idi Amin. McCartney met Fraser when he ran a gallery on Duke Street in London's Grosvenor Square—a spot raided in 1966 for hosting a show authorities deemed obscene. The notoriety only enhanced Fraser's reputation. Paul described the gallery owner as "one of the most influential people of the London sixties scene" and the first person to ever induce him to try cocaine. Through Fraser, the Beatles and the Rolling Stones intermingled with avant-garde sculptor Claes Oldenburg, pop artist Andy Warhol, underground filmmaker Kenneth Anger, and Beat Generation author William Burroughs. Known as Groovy Bob, Fraser was the one who directed the Beatles toward Peter Blake, the artist whose collage design graced the *Sgt. Pepper's Lonely Hearts Club Band* cover. Fraser was also likely the character for which the song "Dr. Robert" was based: "Dr. Robert, he's a man you must believe / Helping everyone in need / No one can succeed like Dr. Robert."

When the Indica Gallery opened, Paul wanted his name associated with it. He already enjoyed the distinction of being the first customer at the Indica Bookshop upstairs, and drew the fliers for the gallery's first show.

On November 9, 1966, Groovy Bob sponsored an exhibit at the Indica. The featured artist was a thirty-three-year-old Japanese woman, now residing in New York.

Like many revolutionaries, Yoko Ono came from a prominent family; her father was descended from the Japanese emperor, while her mother was the granddaughter of Yasuda Zenjiro, founder of the Yasuda Bank (later the Fuji Bank, then the Mizuho Financial Group). But the aftermath of World War II humbled the family. Yoko's father was incarcerated. Other survivors of the fire-bombing of Tokyo seemed to relish the once-powerful Onos' unfortunate circumstances, mocking Yoko's mother as she was forced to beg and barter for food. The experience instilled in Yoko an edge that enabled her to weather the detestation of Beatles fans and, more importantly, to relate to John.

When Yoko was eighteen, the family relocated to affluent Scarsdale, New York. She attended Sarah Lawrence College, then moved to Manhattan and immersed herself in a bohemian lifestyle, using her Lower East Side loft as a performance space. Yoko is credited with playing a significant role in launching Fluxus, an international movement questioning the accepted principles of art and music, blending various creative disciplines. In 1956, she married Japanese composer and pianist Toshi Ichiyanagi in New York. But after she agreed to return to Japan with him, she felt restricted by the society's rigid rules and lack of diversity, and reportedly attempted suicide.

While recovering, she started a relationship with jazz musician Tony Cox, father of Yoko's daughter, Kyoko. Cox and Yoko were not a good match; he was known for wild mood swings, and the two were said to have threatened each other with knives. As with John later on, Cox agreed to be the child's full-time caregiver as well as Yoko's promoter as she continued to confront the sensibilities of the art world. She made a film of the bare derrieres of 365 different people and another of a fly crawling over the body of a nude woman. She also covered one of Trafalgar Square's four bronze lions with enormous white sheets.

John Lennon was curious enough to attend Yoko's Indica opening. But as he walked through the gallery, he was unimpressed.

A bag of carpenter's nails was on sale for 100 British pounds, a fresh apple on a stand for 200. "I thought, 'This is a con. What the hell is this?'" John told the BBC. "I'm expecting an orgy...and it's all quiet."

Because of his celebrity, John was immediately introduced to the artist. Lennon was accustomed to women flirting and trying to impress him. But Yoko seemed to live in a universe that the Beatles hadn't penetrated. As a relative of a monarch said to be of divine origin, Yoko clearly regarded Lennon as a mortal, unsmilingly handing him a card that said, "Breathe."

Mildly amused, John inhaled and exhaled.

Looking around the room, John noticed a white ladder leading toward a white canvas suspended from the ceiling. Ascending the stairwell, Lennon lifted a magnifying glass dangling from a chain and stared at a tiny word on the canvas: YES.

"If it said 'no,' or something nasty like 'rip-off,' or whatever, I would have left the gallery," he told television host Dick Cavett. "Because it was positive, it said 'yes,' I thought, 'Okay, it's the first show I've been to that's said something warm to me.' Then, I decided to see the rest of the show."

Next, Yoko asked John to hammer a nail into a board. The cost of the experience: sixty shillings. John hesitated, then smirked, "Well, I'll give you an imaginary five shillings and hammer an imaginary nail in.'"

Yoko locked eyes with the Beatle. She understood his abstract sense of humor, and liked it.

At the end of the night, both went their separate ways. But John and Yoko continued to communicate, and met on occasion. "It's a teacher-pupil relationship," he told *Playboy*. "I'm the famous one who's supposed to know everything, but she's my teacher."

Yoko told the magazine that she also learned from John. Yet she believed that her "feminine strength" had an impact on the Beatle: "I think women really have the inner wisdom and they're carrying that. . . . Men never developed the inner wisdom—they didn't have time. So most men do rely on women's inner wisdom."

Be that as it might, John seemed to derive little self-awareness from his marriage to Cynthia. While she raised Julian, John was in the midst of a self-centered self-exploration campaign, filling his mind with works by authors he hadn't taken seriously at school— George Orwell, Oscar Wilde, and Leo Tolstoy, among others—or gazing at patterns and colors while tripping on LSD. Although he rarely drew in Cynthia or Julian, he had mentioned Yoko to his wife—her art, her vibrancy, her unique way of thinking. Despite their mutual art school background, Cynthia felt that John viewed her as a local girl from a place he'd outgrown. "He needed more encouragement and support for his way-out ideas," she recounted in her 1978 memoir, *A Twist of Lennon*.

Eventually, Cynthia met Yoko. Outwardly, Cynthia appeared to have nothing to worry about; most of John's friends would have deemed her the more attractive of the two. Yet Cynthia could feel the connection that her husband shared with the Japanese artist. For years, Cynthia had done her best to look the other way while parades of groupies swarmed the Beatles in every city. But the notion of John's association with Yoko filled her with far greater unease.

During one argument, Cynthia voiced her concern, telling John he'd probably be better off with Yoko. John replied that his wife was being delusional.

They both knew better.

■ ■ ■

Initially, the media loved the Beatles because all four members seemed to speak without premeditation. Certainly, Brian Epstein schooled the boys on stage presentation. But the music came from the band, and the unfiltered quotes the Beatles delivered felt authentic and refreshing—until one important section of the American population viciously turned against them.

"I...open my mouth," John told *Rolling Stone*, "something happens."

In this case, John had done more than tweak conservative sensibilities. When he went to introduce a song at concerts and instead looked upwards, scrunching his face, twisting his fingers and shouting out gibberish in a menacing voice, few realized that he was imitating Adolf Hitler. When he stuck a comb under his nose and thrust his arm into the air on a hotel balcony, it was apparent that he was mocking the way the hordes venerated the Beatles with the zeal that others had shown toward the Führer. In essence, there was something valid about Lennon's playacting—a message that no individual, or group of musicians, warranted blind exaltation.

The problem was that John was equally skeptical about religion; Cynthia had had to baptize Julian behind her husband's back. "Christianity will go," he told Maureen Cleave of London's *Evening Standard* in 1966. "It will vanish and shrink. I needn't argue about that. I'm right and I will be proved right. We're more popular than Jesus now. I don't know which will go first, rock 'n' roll or Christianity. Jesus was all right, but his disciples were thick and ordinary. It's them twisting it that ruins it for me."

The quote received little attention in the United Kingdom. However, four months later, an American teen magazine called *Datebook* included the quotes under a headline suggesting that Lennon thought the Beatles were better than Jesus.

The segment of America that would later be labeled the Christian right was incensed, and the backlash swift. Twenty-two radio stations announced a Beatles ban—even though those particular outlets had never played one song by the group in the past. Around the American South, young people were encouraged to burn their "Beatle trash," hurling albums and memorabilia into bonfires.

With another U.S. tour less than two weeks away, there was talk of assassination attempts and Ku Klux Klan rallies. To blunt the impact, Brian Epstein held a press conference in New York. He was conciliatory but firm: although some indelicate language had been used, the Beatles were, and would remain, a cultural phenomenon.

"If any of the promoters were so concerned that a concert should be canceled," he said, "I wouldn't, in fact, stand in their way. Apparently, the Memphis concert...sold more tickets yesterday than they had until that day."

In other words, even in the Deep South—in Elvis's hometown, in fact—the Beatles were king.

On August 11, the day before the tour was slated to kick off at the International Amphitheatre, the Beatles held another press conference at Chicago's Astor Towers Hotel. John believed that the anti-Beatle forces had always hated rock 'n' roll because of its African-American roots and sexuality. Still, he was truly frightened that his words had irreparably damaged Beatlemania—to the point that he and his bandmates might soon be playing the same circuit as Ringo's old stand-in, Jimmy Nicol. In the hotel suite before the conference, he broke down and cried. Then he went out and took responsibility for the miscommunication. His point, he re-emphasized, was that it seemed that the Beatles

> meant more to kids than Jesus did or religion at that time. I wasn't knocking it or putting it down. I was just saying it as a fact....I'm not saying that we're better or greater or comparing us with Jesus Christ as a person or god or a thing or whatever it is. I just said what I said, and it was wrong or it was taken wrong. And now, it's all this.

He elaborated that he'd felt comfortable with the reporter, and that his comments had been based on his interpretation of numerous books on Christianity: "I was using expressions on things that I'd just read and derived about Christianity, only I was saying it in the simplest form that I know, which is the natural way I talk."

But was he sorry, the reporters wanted to know. Lennon seemed to bristle when asked the question but—considering all that could be lost if he remained obstinate—came through with an apology. To the rebellious youth starting to view Lennon as their spokesman, John had maintained his credibility. To mostly everyone else, he'd expressed enough contrition to receive forgiveness.

■　■　■

Mark Chapman was in high school when he lost his admiration for John.

Chapman had been amused by the "more popular than Jesus" story, until his worldview dramatically changed a few years later. The metamorphosis occurred after a group of strangers stole his wallet. No longer convinced that drugs could protect him from the mercilessness of the world, sixteen-year-old Chapman searched for something more genuine, more permanent. On this occasion, he turned not to the little people, but to tradition. Twisting his palms heavenward, he declared, "Jesus, come to me. Come help me."

Instantly, he was filled with the spirit, and redirected his life. Chapman cut his hair and threw away his Army jacket. Church activities replaced the monotony of hanging out and getting wasted. When the young man was seen on the street, he was generally handing out religious pamphlets. At Columbia High School, he walked the hallways holding a Bible and a "Jesus notebook" that included jottings about his newfound faith.

Like many who become suddenly religious, he was intolerant of anyone who threatened the cause. In his mind, one of the greatest culprits was John Lennon.

Chapman destroyed his Beatles records. The lyrics to "Imagine" were examined and critiqued.

John spoke about imagining no possessions, yet here he was, living the life of a multimillionaire, buying property all over the world, scorning people like Chapman, who'd been naïve enough to perceive the Beatle as the working-class hero he sang about.

Lennon was a phony.

"Imagine there's no heaven." How could John Lennon say something like this? It meant that he didn't believe in God, and wanted others to also consider the atheistic path.

Friends said that Chapman changed the words to the song, spouting instead, "Imagine if John were dead."

■   ■   ■

As the Beatles turned away from western belief systems, the Maharishi launched into their orbit, bringing with him a form of faith that was just as offensive to Chapman. Technically, Maharishi Mahesh Yogi, a mocha-skinned guru with a tuft of gray in an otherwise black beard, was supposed to help the group shed outside distractions, including drugs. But the founder of Transcendental Meditation had become a celebrity himself, driving around in a Rolls Royce while lecturing moneyed adherents about his "new religious movement."

For the most part, the Beatles needed an escape from Beatlemania. With the exception of Ringo—who enjoyed traveling first class, being picked up at airports, and having access to endless funds—the lads were emotionally wrecked. Generally, fads like the cult of the Fab Four flamed out, but Beatlemania only continued to escalate. Unable to walk the streets, John complained of sitting in his hotel room, overeating and drinking himself into a stupor. Although his childhood had been unhappy and largely unfulfilling, he found himself longing for the simplicity and anonymity expressed in the song "Help!": "Now these days are gone, I'm not so self-assured, / Now I find I've changed my mind and opened up the doors."

Perhaps because of his secondary role in the band, George appeared to be the first Beatle to truly detest Beatlemania. "Of course, at first we all thought we wanted the fame and that," he said at a launch party for his 1987 album, *Cloud Nine*. "But, very shortly thereafter, we began to think twice....After the initial excitement and thrill wore off, I, for one, became depressed. Is this all we have to look forward to in life—being chased around by a crowd of hooting lunatics from one crappy hotel room to the next?"

Although his fellow Beatles would later herald his writing talents—and none less than Frank Sinatra declared Harrison's ballad "Something" the finest love song in a half century—George was bitter that he had to fight the Lennon-McCartney axis to get a tune on a Beatle album. "The problem was that John and Paul had written songs for so long...they had such a lot of tunes and they automatically thought that theirs should be priority," George told *Crawdaddy* magazine. "So for me, I'd always have to wait through ten of their songs before they'd even listen to one of mine....I had a little encouragement from time to time, but it was very little. It was like they were doing me a favor."

Still, George's contemporaries outwardly recognized his influence on the Beatles. Keith Richards told *People* magazine, "We held similar positions in our respective bands, which formed a special, knowing bond between us."

Overshadowed by Mick Jagger, Richards' followers identified him as the heart of the Rolling Stones. Likewise, it was George who largely took the Beatles down their psychedelic path, viewing his early LSD use as a retreat from the mediocrity of both his Catholic childhood and the superficial hit-making industry. Under the influence of acid, George not only deciphered music differently, but asked questions about the essence of life itself.

John had also become a seeker and, initially, shared his bandmate's passion for synthetic experimentation. While attending a party in Hollywood, actor Peter Fonda showed Harrison and Lennon a wound from a childhood gunshot accident. This wasn't the type of acid trip George envisioned, and he became agitated and scared.

"I know what it's like to be dead," Fonda boasted.

John had too much knowledge of real people dying to indulge the actor. "Listen, mate," he cut in, "shut up about that stuff."

Retorted Fonda, "You're making me feel like I've never been born."

On the song "She Said She Said," John transformed Fonda into a female character: "She said, 'I know what's it's like to be dead' / …And she's making me feel like I've never been born."

The track appeared on *Revolver*, an album that featured such acid-induced devices as a guitar solo played backwards and John's voice running through a rotating Leslie speaker, usually used only with the Hammond organ. But George possessed the awareness to sense that one couldn't rely on substance abuse to realize all of life's truths. So in 1966, he began traveling to India, spending six weeks studying sitar with Ravi Shankar, and seeking spiritual guidance from the Maharishi, embracing his basic message of positive thinking to benefit the individual and the world at large.

Despite George's role in the shadows of Lennon and McCartney, the Beatles opened themselves up to the Maharishi's teachings, leading other celebrities on the mystical journey. Actress Mia Farrow called George "a spiritual force."

Prior to the Beatles, folk singers like Woody Guthrie, Joan Baez and Pete Seeger were generally the only musicians comfortable speaking out on controversial topics like war and civil rights. Within the band, there was some debate over whether to follow Epstein's counsel not to even offer opinions on soccer, or satiate the hunger of those who wanted the Beatles to guide them.

In 1966—a year that found 385,000 American troops in Vietnam, and a portion of the country enraged by John Lennon's infamous Jesus remarks—the Beatles proclaimed that they favored peace. While the members alleged that all the hero worship had become a burden, they accepted that their words had impact, not only on fans in their general age bracket, but younger ones, like Mark David Chapman.

These were the kind of people the Beatles hoped would lead their peers down the path of non-violence.

As the Maharishi preached, one person's deeds could change the world.

9

PORTRAIT OF A CRAZY MAN

Like many teens discovering *The Catcher in the Rye* for the first time, Mark David Chapman related to the way that Holden Caulfield saw adult priorities as meaningless, and teachers, parents, and politicians as hypocrites and charlatans. Unaware that thousands of young people felt exactly the same way, Chapman began to see himself as Holden, the lone voice against an unjust society.

Interestingly, Chapman's enthrallment with *The Catcher in the Rye* occurred during a period when he was happy. Surrounded by other young Christians who treated him as a friend, Chapman thrived. While working as a counselor at a YMCA summer camp, Mark was nicknamed "Nemo" by the children, and named Outstanding Counselor. As he was handed the award, the kids leaped to their feet, chanting, "Ne-mo, Ne-mo, Ne-mo."

Chapman's bosses noticed, and appointed him assistant director.

"He had real leadership qualities," Tony Adams, the former executive director of the South DeKalb YMCA told *New York* magazine. "Mark was a very caring person. Hate was not even in his vocabulary. . . . He felt like the Lord had touched him. . . . He wanted to prove that he was a good person."

After high school graduation, Chapman moved to Chicago, where he was again embraced by his fellow Christians, playing guitar at churches and other spiritual gatherings while his friend Michael McFarland amused the crowd with impersonations.

The YMCA's international program sent Mark to Lebanon, but he soon found himself in the midst of the civil war between

Christians and Muslims. Evacuated with the rest of the YMCA's staff, he came back to the States a stronger person with real-world experience—a young man who'd rested on his Christian faith with the boom of bombs and crackle of machine gun fire in the distance. He was given another assignment, working at a resettlement camp with young Vietnamese refugees at Fort Chaffee, Arkansas. Very quickly, Chapman was appointed an area coordinator. When President Gerald Ford visited, Mark was introduced to the commander-in-chief and shook his hand.

The same year, Ford survived two separate assassination attempts. But neither the president nor his Secret Service agents ever sensed from Chapman that the popular twenty-year-old posed any sort of danger.

Mark's roommate at the time, David Moore, told the New York *Daily News*, "He was one of the most compassionate staff members we had.... He cared.... He had a real sensibility for kids."

At night, Moore and Chapman opened their Bibles and had rewarding discussions about living their Christian principles. Every Sunday, they attended church, often with Chapman's girlfriend, Jessica Blankenship. "I think that was the high point of his life," she told NBC's *Dateline* program. "I fell in love with him, and I think he fell in love with me, too."

What impressed Jessica the most was the way Chapman interacted with the Vietnamese children. As at the summer camp, he knew exactly how to reach them. "I thought, 'Wow, he really has a gift,'" she recounted. "'If he treats children like that, then this is looking good.'"

In her private moments, she envisioned herself married to Chapman and living in the suburbs, surrounded by a brood of happy children.

Unfortunately, Mark's private moments were very different. Although his Christian beliefs had propelled him further than anyone ever guessed, the darkness of the period when he'd dropped acid and run away from home never quite faded.

One morning in 1975, Mark's friend from Georgia, Miles McManus, received a package in the mail. Inside was a cassette tape. Miles clicked it into his recorder and heard Chapman's familiar voice.

"Hello, and welcome to the Mark Chapman Tape."

Thus far, everything seemed normal. Without e-mail or Skype, this was the high-tech option in 1975 for young people striving for a connection more immediate than a letter. Chapman told his friend about his music tastes. Although he'd grown disenchanted with Lennon, he still idolized Todd Rundgren, he said. The artist's song "An Elpee's Worth of Toons," in particular, expressed the way Chapman viewed himself: "A portrait of a crazy man...a picture of a soul in pain."

■ ■ ■

In a four-year period, the Beatles had played more than 1,400 concerts, averaging some 350 shows annually. "It got a little boring," John said of the relentless touring to television host Tom Snyder. "We just became like lip-synching mimes."

All four of the Beatles were known to complain that they couldn't hear each other over all the screaming and were thus unable to grow professionally on stage. In the studio, the Beatles had taken bold steps forward, creating elaborate works like "Eleanor Rigby" and "Tomorrow Never Knows." But, given the primordial concert equipment available at the time, it was all but impossible to perform these songs at a typical Beatles show.

On August 29, 1966, the Beatles played their last official concert at Candlestick Park in San Francisco, where, ironically, a whole different music scene was sprouting—aroused by the artists' contempt for the conformity that had settled in the American West, and fed with a liberal allocation of psychedelics. Paul was uncomfortable with the finality of the decision, convinced of the importance of maintaining contact between the Beatles and their fans.

From Epstein's perspective, the band was closing the spigot on a crucial revenue stream. But the Beatles, and the world they'd affected, had changed greatly in the four years since Brian fired Pete Best and mandated that the lads wear suits. As Epstein battled his own demons, he could no longer count on the band he'd made famous to heed his instructions.

They were the Beatles, with or without him.

■   ■   ■

Chapman stood on Seventy-second Street, pondering the flash he'd seen earlier in the day of a man getting into a taxi. Had it been Lennon? Chapman believed it must have been. But now word had spread among the Dakota regulars that John was back in the building. Mark knew that he'd left his post a few times, and wondered if John had managed to get back inside without passing him.

Upstairs, John and Yoko were being interviewed by California radio personality Dave Sholin for a segment scheduled to air on the RKO network. The interview centered on *Double Fantasy*, and on the challenges of marriage and of raising Sean. Sholin knew how well the album was doing and, as an industry insider, understood that the demands on the couple were increasing. As a result, he expected the Lennons to feel pressured to get through the interview and move on to another commitment. But they were completely relaxed, and the exchange became more a conversation than an interview. Time went quickly, and Sholin was in the Lennon apartment for approximately three hours.

"I'm really talking to the people who grew up with me," Lennon said of the album. "I'm saying, 'Here I am now. How are you? How's your relationship going? Did you get through it all? Wasn't the seventies a drag? Here we are. Let's try to make it through the eighties.'"

Before his sabbatical, John noted, he'd supported a lot of causes—some out of passion, others out of curiosity, a few more because he needed to reassess his value system and grow up. However, John and Yoko's fundamental message—that every individual needed to embrace peace and spread it to the world—remained unaltered.

"I still believe in love, peace," he told Sholin. "I still believe in positive thinking. We're trying to imagine there's no wars—to live that love and peace rather than sing about it only."

Even at his best, John always seemed to have death on his mind—and five years of serenity with his wife and child couldn't change that. "We're going to live or we're going to die," he said. "If we're dead, we're going to have to deal with that. If we're alive, we're going to have to deal with being alive. So worrying about whether Wall Street or the Apocalypse is going to come in the form of the Great Beast isn't going to do us any good today."

Only later would every sentence John articulated that afternoon be scrutinized for its poignancy. "I hope I die before Yoko," he said, "because, if Yoko died, I wouldn't know how to survive. I couldn't carry on."

He didn't dwell on the topic for long. He and his fans had lived through some unbridled years, and he was grateful to emerge from the other end with them: "We all survived.... The whole map's changed and we're going into an unknown future, but we're all still here.

"And while there's life, there's still hope."

After turning his back on the music industry, the *Double Fantasy* experience—along with John and Yoko's recent forays in the studio—had renewed John's creativity. As much as he sang about the merry-go-round of celebrity, he was having fun making records—more fun than he'd ever had in the Beatles—and promoting them.

"I consider that my work won't be finished until I'm dead and buried," he told Sholin, "and I hope that's a long time."

The journey to this stage had been a shaky one. In 1960, John never could have predicted that, on a sunny, tranquil day in 1980, he'd be entertaining a friendly reporter in his New York home with his Japanese wife. So he wasn't about to offer prognostications for the next few decades. But he was confident, he claimed, because he and Yoko felt great.

As he put it, they were "wild about life."

■   ■   ■

Before the Beatles played their last show, work had already begun on rock 'n' roll's first full-blown concept album, *Sgt. Pepper's Lonely Hearts Club Band*. As with the Kinks' *The Village Green Preservation Society* later on, there was a nostalgic element to the project, a sense of mourning for a way of life that was changing quickly—largely because of the Beatles themselves. The notion of a band wandering the countryside bringing cheer to the lonely harked back to an age when entertainment was primarily delivered face to face. The lyrics of "Being for the Benefit of Mr. Kite" were taken almost verbatim from a poster John had purchased, advertising a nineteenth-century event promoted by Pablo Fanque, the first British circus owner of African origin. Disregarding the psychedelic elements, there was even something wholesome about "Lucy in the Sky with Diamonds."

The inspiration occurred one day when Julian Lennon came home from preschool, holding a drawing. Although John was later depicted as an indifferent father, he always looked forward to seeing his four-year-old son's paintings and illustrations. Because of Julian's artwork, John explored interests from his own child-hood, particularly Lewis Carroll's *Through the Looking-Glass*—an influence behind "I Am the Walrus," among other songs. As soon as John spotted the diamond-shaped eyes on the character in Julian's picture, he asked the boy about it.

"It's Lucy in the sky with diamonds," Julian explained, referring to a little girl in his class named Lucy O'Donnell.

Initially, Lennon had hoped to include "Strawberry Fields Forever" on the album. But because *Sgt. Pepper's Lonely Hearts Club*

Band was already loaded up, the tune about longing for the days of romping in Liverpool's Strawberry Fields was pushed onto *Magical Mystery Tour.* "We were trying to write about Liverpool," John told *Rolling Stone* in 1968, "and I just listed all the nice-sounding names, just arbitrarily.... I mean, I have visions of Strawberry Fields. And there was Penny Lane and the Cast Iron Shore ... and they were just good names, just groovy names, just good-sounding. Because Strawberry Fields is anywhere you want to go."

As tender as it sounded, though, there were always pangs of sadness in Lennon's work. The line "no one I think is in my tree" was John's way of recalling his melancholy over his belief that nobody understood him.

■ ■ ■

When *Sgt. Pepper's Lonely Hearts Club Band* was finally released in 1967, John, Paul, George, and Ringo had each undergone a makeover, popping off the cover in living color, sporting facial hair. John's glasses—the circular variety issued by Britain's National Health department—became stylish, simply because they rested on his nose. The cover design highlighted the Beatles—in fluorescent satin uniforms reminiscent of the Salvation Army—in front of cutouts of such personalities as Sigmund Freud, Karl Marx, Marilyn Monroe, Lewis Carroll, Bob Dylan, and former Liverpool footballer Albert Stubbins. To Lennon's right stood the dark-suited, mop-topped Beatles of 1964 vintage, stooped forward, resembling—depending on the interpreter—wax figures or ghosts.

Lennon had asked that Jesus Christ also be included in the montage. But after the album burnings south of the Mason-Dixon line, the concept was vetoed.

Hidden in the glare of the post-Beatlemania Beatles were Lennon's lyrics, still digging into his soul to express painful self-truths. Despite the fact that he'd soon hurt Cynthia in a humiliating, public manner, John offered regret over his longstanding attitudes towards women. On "Getting Better," for instance—a song inspired by a phrase Jimmy Nicol frequently uttered during his short stint with the Beatles—Lennon acknowledged: "I used to be cruel to my woman / I beat her and kept her apart from the things that she loved."

"All that...was me," he later told *Playboy*. "I used to be cruel to my women, and physically....I was a hitter. I couldn't express myself and hit. I fought men and I hit women. That is why I am always on about peace, you see. It is the most violent people who go for love and peace. Everything's the opposite."

■　　■　　■

Still stationed in front of the Dakota, waiting for John to come out, Mark Chapman felt the bulge of the gun in his jacket and fingered the pages of *The Catcher in the Rye*. Despite his mission, he'd made no effort to keep his obsession with John Lennon a secret; fans showed up at the building all the time, and there was nothing about Chapman's appearance or manner that made him stand out. During a previous trip, just over a month ago, he'd wandered outside the building, spoken to the doorman, and looked up to see if he could detect John or Yoko in a window. Chapman couldn't even figure out which windows belonged to the famous couple. And even if the former Beatle had come outside and introduced himself, there was another factor preventing Chapman from following through on his fantasy.

New York City law barred someone from just coming in off the street and purchasing bullets for a .38 Charter Arms revolver.

Now, he was back again, and fully prepared. He'd initially checked into the YMCA, but didn't want the press reporting that Chapman was crashing in a $16.50-a-night room, next door to druggies and sexual deviants. The Sheraton was where he belonged. The desk clerk and bellmen called him "sir." And when he walked through the lobby, nobody looked at him as anything but an honored guest.

Even the cabbies treated him like a big shot. When he'd hailed a taxi in front of the Dakota over the weekend, the driver cocked the wheel quickly to pick him up. The cabbie didn't say it, but Chapman wondered if the man thought that he was chauffeuring a resident. It didn't seem so far-fetched, Chapman thought, him living in the same building as John Lennon.

"Where you going?"

"Greenwich Village."

The cabbie directed the vehicle downtown.

"Man, I've been busy," Chapman offered.

"What do you do?"

"I'm a recording engineer. And I've been working on...you have to promise not to tell anybody."

The cabbie nodded.

"It's a special project. Paul McCartney and John Lennon are getting back together. That was John Lennon's place I was coming from. I'm the engineer."

■　　■　　■

On August 24, 1967, the Maharishi held a lecture on Transcendental Meditation in London, and three of the Beatles were there to publicize the event and the movement. George attended with his wife, Patti, Paul with girlfriend Jane Asher, and John with Cynthia. The next day, a swarm of reporters turned up at Euston Station to see all four Beatles, along with Mick Jagger and Marianne Faithfull, board a train to Bangor, Wales for a seminar. It was a disorderly scene, and Cynthia became separated from John. As the train rolled out of the station, the photographers spun around to focus on Mrs. Lennon, in tears on the platform.

She later said that this was the moment when she realized that she was about to be ditched.

Brian Epstein had promised to join the Beatles after he took care of business in London, leasing the Saville Theatre for a Jimi Hendrix concert. But while the Beatles were with the Maharishi,

Brian's housekeeper noticed that he hadn't opened the bedroom door all day. Feeling concerned, she called his name, knocked and finally entered the room, discovering the body of the thirty-two-year-old manager.

For his entire adult life, Brian's success—both at building his father's businesses and at crafting the Beatles into a merchandising machine—was counteracted by his shame over his sexual orientation. As the Beatles experimented with an assortment of drugs, Epstein pursued his own vices, losing thousands of pounds a night in gambling clubs, and becoming addicted to amphetamines and other pills. On tour, the group members often didn't know where Epstein went at night, but noticed that he appeared depressed. Two weeks before he died, a reporter from *Melody Maker* magazine asked Brian about his greatest fear.

"Loneliness," he responded. "...Although, actually, one inflicts loneliness on oneself to a certain extent."

During the *Sgt. Pepper's Lonely Hearts Club Band* recording sessions, Brian checked himself into a clinic. Upon his release, though, he was immediately thrust back into the less than temperate climate created by the Beatles, at the peak of their psychedelic phase. In order to fall asleep each night, his sedative of choice was Carbitral. His tolerance was so high that he'd generally consume up to six pills, a dose that doctors claimed bordered on the toxic.

A post-mortem examination revealed that Brian died of an accidental overdose of sleeping pills, although to this day many believe that—as the Beatles grew up and started going their own way—the self-destructive manager wished to put himself out of his misery.

After several days of the Maharishi's lectures, the normally skeptical Lennon told the press that his meditation had instilled a "confidence to stand such a shock." Harrison, the Beatle most smitten with the mystical, reiterated his belief that there was "no such thing as death, only in the physical sense. We know he is okay now. He will return because he was striving for happiness, and desired bliss so much."

Ironically, less than one month after Epstein's death, homosexual relations were legalized in England, a first step toward alleviating the kind of inner torment Brian experienced. John's enduring gift to his manager was the song "You've Got to Hide Your Love Away," performed by the man many believed to be Brian's symbol of obsession on twelve-string guitar.

■   ■   ■

A week from now, everyone would know Mark David Chapman's name.

The thought excited Chapman. This was his third day outside the Dakota, and something big was coming. But did he really have the nerve to kill Lennon? Maybe he could do something else, a feat so unexpected it might have the same impact. Mark began to feel that he didn't care if he lost his life. If a cop shot him as he was gunning down John, that was okay—as long as Lennon died, too, and Chapman was immortalized as the killer.

But what if he didn't see Lennon? All the other fans outside the Dakota had spotted the Beatle. After two trips to New York, why hadn't Mark? Maybe this wasn't what Chapman was meant to do.

Still, Mark knew that he wasn't leaving New York. And he wouldn't die a nobody. If he didn't kill John, he had other ideas—like going to the crown of the Statue of Liberty with the other tourists, then jumping off.

People would remember him for that.

■   ■   ■

While the Beatles and their celebrity friends were studying Transcendental Meditation with Mahrishi Mahesh Yogi at a retreat in Rishikesh, India, the guru apparently cornered Mia Farrow in a dark cave and clumsily threw his arms her. Paul and Ringo had already returned to England by this stage, but, when the story—

along with a tale about the Maharishi seducing another female follower—reached John and George, they confronted the alleged "celibate ascetic" about it. John noted that George seemed uncertain about their spiritual guide's integrity, and his own faith in the Maharishi dissolved. As John was leaving India, he started to pen a new song: "Maharishi, what have you done? / You made a fool of everyone."

Farrow later said that she might have misinterpreted the gesture, and George came to see the Maharishi as the victim of a series of malicious rumors. Lennon wasn't so certain, but he acquiesced when Harrison insisted on purging the spiritualist's name from the song—titling it instead "Sexy Sadie."

A month after the India debacle, Cynthia Lennon was traveling in Greece, and John decided to invite Yoko to his home, ostensibly to tape-record experimental music. When Cynthia returned home, she found John and Yoko sitting cross-legged on the floor, staring into one another's eyes. Yoko had also placed her slippers outside John and Cynthia's bedroom door. Essentially, the Japanese artist had moved in. John offered no apologies, and Cynthia packed her bags.

Interestingly, she didn't fault the couple for falling in love, believing that they possessed a "unity of mind and body" that she could never match. "Yoko did not take John away from me," Cynthia wrote in her autobiography, *A Twist of Lennon*, "because he had never been mine. He had always been his own man, and had always done his own thing."

Nonetheless, she had no choice but to sue John for divorce, on the grounds of adultery. John didn't contest, and on November 8, 1968, the divorce was finalized.

■   ■   ■

George Arzt bounded up the Renaissance Revival-style stairs into City Hall. His quarters in the building were modest, but better than those of his colleagues in the filthy *New York Post* newsroom, with the peeling paint and broken typewriters. In the past, his bosses had expected him to check in as soon as he arrived at Herald Square on the F train from Queens. Fishing in his pocket for coins, George would find a pay phone and ask about his assignment for the day. When nothing was going on, he'd be told to report to City Hall. After years of hearing the same thing day after day, somehow George turned from a general assignment reporter into the *Post's* City Hall bureau chief.

Even in 1980, a significant number of the New York press corps were guys who might have ended up in civil service. At the *Post* and *Daily News* in particular, the reporters tended to come from the outer boroughs, and to write with a blue-collar sensibility. George remembered his own mother telling him in Yiddish, "Whatever you become is up to you. Because we don't have any money to help you."

He was initially attracted to newspaper work because he'd been shy, and believed that the process of asking questions would make him more sociable. Now he loved the whole lifestyle. He'd worked alongside the greats of New York City journalism—Jimmy Breslin, Pete Hamill, Nora Ephron, Helen Dudar. As sexist as reporters could be, if a woman was tough and good, she was one of the boys. And City Hall was a great beat to cover. In the mid-seventies, when Abe Beame was mayor—and the city was experiencing its first serious layoffs since the Great Depression—you had to be careful about what you said in the City Hall Blue Room. Reporters were warned not to use the word "bankruptcy" in front of the mayor. You could say that the city was "seemingly on the brink of the abyss," but never bankrupt. Ed Koch was a different kind of administrator. You could utter anything you wanted, as long as you were prepared for an agitated and personal rebuttal.

Celebrities and statesmen passed through City Hall every day. And just being out on the streets covering stories created more potential for spotting the famous. Unlike some of his colleagues, George had never experienced a John Lennon sighting. But he had seen Yoko Ono a few times. Despite the detachment reporters were expected to display, Yoko's association with the Beatles intrigued him. He admired the group, first as pop stars, then as innovators creating new sounds and proposing concepts he'd never considered before.

"They just tussled my middle-class background," he said.

Ten years earlier, when the Beatles broke up, George was shattered. He compared it to that heartrending moment when the Brooklyn Dodgers moved to Los Angeles at the end of the 1957 season.

■　■　■

At about 2:30 P.M., Chapman noticed a smiling child, with brown hair and a hint of an Asiatic strain, ambling toward the Dakota with a nanny. Jude Stein, one of the female regulars outside the building, approached Sean Lennon and asked him about his day. Sean appeared to be familiar with Jude, and showed her his hand.

"I banged my finger in the door."

"It doesn't look so bad. You'll be okay."

Chapman walked away from Paul Goresh to join the conversation. Jude glanced over. Mark appeared to be a calm, friendly man.

"Oh, isn't he a cute, sweet boy?" Chapman said, leaning forward and extending his hand. Sean looked up and happily accepted the handshake.

■　■　■

Brian Epstein's brother, Clive, was called into emergency service to manage the Beatles. But Clive did not have the same fervor for the Beatles as his sibling, and the group's relationships with several old business associates soon fell apart. Paul attempted to drive the band artistically. *Magical Mystery Tour* was an undisciplined effort to capture the Beatles' spontaneity on celluloid as the group rode around on a bus—interspersed with the 1967 equivalent of music videos—accompanied by a cast of characters that included John's

Uncle Charlie. But nothing interesting ever really occurred, and the ambitious project failed.

Nonetheless, some of the Beatles' greatest music appeared on the *Magical Mystery Tour* album, including "Penny Lane," "The Fool on the Hill," "Strawberry Fields Forever," and "I Am the Walrus"—a dreamy, mildly disturbing venture into the mind of John Lennon. The cinematic performance of the song—featuring the Beatles in egg and animal costumes; swaying, hand-holding English bobbies; and a montage of faces from an earlier age—accomplished its goal of taking the viewer into the realm of the surreal, and maintained its vanguard status decades later.

Another song on the album represented John's aspirations for humanity as much as "Imagine." The Beatles debuted the tune shortly before Brian's death—on the first live, satellite television program beamed around the world. Appropriately titled *Our World*, the show reached more than 350 million people on five continents. Faced with the challenge of communicating a single, uncomplicated theme to viewers from a multitude of cultures, the Beatles—with friends like Mick Jagger, Keith Moon, Eric Clapton and Graham Nash rocking side to side in the studio—declared, "All You Need Is Love."

■   ■   ■

Chapman's encounter with Sean Lennon had been a heart-thumping break in a tedious afternoon. After the boy left, Chapman began chatting with Jude Stein. Jude knew the Lennons well and was a true Beatles expert. Mark enjoyed listening to her speak, and told her about his way of life in Hawaii. Both were chilly at this point, so Chapman asked Jude to join him for something to eat at a nearby restaurant.

Many of the stores on Columbus Avenue had photos of John Lennon in the window. He'd visited each one and engaged in some type of dialogue with the staff. Chapman could tell that John appealed not only to Beatles fans, but the people who saw him day to day. He treated his neighbors nicely, and they liked him. Back in YMCA camp, Mark had been similarly regarded. But what about his neighbors now, in Hawaii? What would they say about him? Some called him quiet; others described him as weird.

Chapman would later contend that he'd asked Jude on a date that night. This was an effort to derail his own plan, he said. Had she consented, it could have changed history. He still might have tried to shoot Lennon, but maybe the next day or the day after that. Because his mind drifted in so many directions, Chapman wondered if he would have been distracted by something else before his next opportunity to commit the crime.

When Jude was interviewed by *Dateline* in 2005, she said that she couldn't remember any romantic overture. Chapman seemed nice, and he liked the Beatles; she had conversations with people like him every time she went to the Dakota. There was nothing more to the exchange.

She was all but certain that he hadn't asked her out: "No way in a million years. That whole statement has to be fabricated in his mind...first I'm hearing of it."

They headed back toward the Dakota, but it was getting colder. "How late are you going to stay?" she asked Chapman.

"I plan to stay as long as it takes."

She assumed he was talking about getting an autograph.

Chapman resumed his position in front of the building, a copy of *Double Fantasy* under his arm. He nodded at the doorman and at Paul Goresh. Jude leaned against the gargoyles on the railing. Upstairs, John was wrapping up his radio interview. John and Yoko needed to get to the studio. He'd gone over her recording of "Walking on Thin Ice" that morning, and knew where adjustments needed to be made. He was feeling confident about the single and had a vision of Yoko commanding the A side of a hit record with his own song on the B side. Minds were opening, he concluded. People—average people—were starting to understand Yoko as an artist, the same way they were opening their hearts to peace.

"To work with your best friend is a joy," he told Dave Sholin. "My best friend is my wife. Who could ask for anything more?"

Downstairs, Chapman began to feel possessed by the devil.

■　■　■

Many of the fans rejoicing over John and Yoko's sentimentality on *Double Fantasy* in 1980 were the same ones who'd initially felt repelled by the sight of them. The sixties had been a bleak, conformist extension of the fifties until John, Paul, George, and Ringo threw open the door, and invited everyone to their party. Then, her critics contended, Yoko burst into the room and started bumming everyone out.

Not long after they consummated their relationship, John and Yoko showed up at an avant-garde jazz show at Cambridge University, and were invited onto the stage. "That was the first time I appeared un-Beatled," John told *Rolling Stone*.

> I just hung around and played feedback, and people got very upset because they recognized me. "What's he doing here?" It's always, "Stay in your bag"...Everybody has pictures they want to live up to. But that's the same as living up to your parents' expectations, or society's expectations....You have to break out of your bag to keep alive.

The more the couple felt resistance, the more they pushed back. Theirs was a public romance, and John knew that all he had to do was materialize somewhere to make a statement. So here were John and Yoko, planting two acorns on the grounds of Coventry Cathedral—one facing east, one west—to represent the merging of their two cultures. Outside the Robert Fraser Gallery, Yoko stood next to John as he cut a string releasing 365 helium balloons. Each was attached with a card declaring, "You Are Here," urging the recipient to write John care of the gallery. When John and Yoko opened the responses, though, they were saddened to discover that most fans wanted him to go back to Cynthia.

One day, the pair encountered a group of young people outside EMI Studios on Abbey Road. A bouquet of yellow roses was passed forward, and Yoko seemed genuinely touched, thanking the fans several times.

Said John, "It's about time someone did something decent to her."

It was only then that the pair realized that Yoko had been deliberately handed the flowers thorns first.

Despite their tough exteriors, the negativity hurt both John and Yoko. "The most humiliating thing is to be looked at as a parasite," she explained to *Playboy*. They loved each other and wanted to help the world, she reasoned. Why couldn't people be happy for them?

"When somebody says something like, 'How can you be with that woman?' you say, 'What do you mean?'" Lennon told the magazine. "Why do you want to throw a rock at her, or punish me for being in love with her?" John's perennial feelings of alienation simmered up, and he began to believe that Yoko was the only person to whom he could turn. He told friends that he couldn't stand to be away from her—even for a couple of minutes.

"To work on this relationship with Yoko is very hard, and we've got the gift of love," he told the Associated TeleVision company (ATV) in England in 1969. "But love is like a precious plant. You can't just accept it and leave it in the cupboard. . . . You gotta keep watering it. You've got to really look after it, and be careful of it, and keep the flies off and see that it's all right, and nurture it."

Over and over, John described himself and Yoko as a single person. He even cracked, "Yoko is me in drag."

Yoko's all-consuming grasp on John rattled the harmony of the Beatles. Paul believed that John now viewed the Beatles as a hindrance to spending time with his girlfriend—like a nine-to-five job, or doing homework. Although Ringo was the most understanding, his wife, Maureen, was close with Cynthia, creating a sense of awkwardness between the drummer and Yoko.

Just as John's divorce with Cynthia was finalized, he and Yoko released their own album, *Two Virgins*, containing the recordings of the squawking and tweeting sounds the couple had made at the house during Cynthia's Greek vacation. On the cover, John and Yoko stood with arms around each other, hair mussed, completely naked. On the back of the album, the pair was also nude, holding hands, peeking over their shoulders at the camera. Clearly, they were not the most beautiful couple in the world, but that was the point.

"We wanted to say, 'We met, we're in love, we want to share it,'" John told Dave Sholin at the Dakota. "And it was kind of a statement, as well, of an awakening for me, too. 'This Beatle thing you've all heard about, this is how I am really.' You know, 'This is me naked, with the woman I love. You want to share it?'"

Paul certainly didn't. "John's in love with Yoko," he said, "and he's no longer in love with the three of us."

■　■　■

At about 5:00 P.M., John and Yoko finally came out of the Dakota.

The interview had gone longer than anyone expected, cutting into time reserved at the studio. Dave Sholin offered to give them a lift.

Mark David Chapman saw the ex-Beatle acknowledge Paul Goresh.

"Paul, have you been here long?"

The two briefly chatted, and Chapman looked at them anxiously. Paul summoned the visitor toward them. John caught Chapman's glance and noticed the copy of *Double Fantasy* in his hands. Chapman held it out.

"You want that signed?"

Chapman felt nervous; after all these years of obsessing over John Lennon, the Beatle was addressing him directly.

"Would you sign my album?" Chapman asked, handing John a black Bic pen.

Goresh stepped back and adjusted his lens, catching a satisfied Chapman peering down at the album as John tried scribbling on the shiny cover. The pen didn't work at first, and John shook it. Yoko stopped and briefly studied Mark. He looked the same as any other fan. It was nice how something as inconsequential as an autograph could bring joy into someone's life.

Finally, the pen was working. John wrote, "John Lennon." Below his name, he added "1980."

Yoko was already in the car, but John lingered a moment longer.

"Is that all you want?"

Chapman sensed that Lennon knew something; perhaps his instincts told him that Mark David Chapman was going to play a dramatic role his life. Otherwise, what would compel him to act so nice?

"His wife was in the car," Chapman recalled to Larry King on CNN. "The door was open, and he's a busy man. He's going to...his record studio, and he's talking to a nobody, and he's asking me is that all I want. I mean, he's giving me the autograph. I don't have a camera on me. What could I give him?"

Mark shook his head from side to side. "No, thank you," he told John.

Lennon turned and joined his wife in the vehicle. The door closed, and Sholin pulled out. It was two weeks until the winter solstice, and the sky was darkening. In the shops they passed, merchants were turning on their Christmas lights. The season seemed to make John giddy. The interview with Sholin was over, but Lennon still felt like talking, enthusiastically reminiscing about Little Richard and other artists he'd idolized as a teenager. Then, he started to sing. "Be-bop-a-lula, she's my baby...."

Lennon even said a few good things about Paul McCartney.

Back at the Dakota, Chapman asked Goresh about the photo: "Did I have my hat on or off in the picture? I wanted my hat off. They'll never believe this in Hawaii."

He walked over to a ledge in front of the building and placed the album there. Doorman Jose Perdomo smiled at him.

"Do me a favor," Chapman said, "and remember where I put that because you'll want to know."

He later claimed to have heard two voices inside his head.

"Let's go home."

"No, no, no. I want to kill him."

■ ■ ■

Yoko and Tony Cox finalized their split in February 1969, and Yoko was granted custody of their daughter, Kyoko. On March 20, John and Yoko married on Gibraltar, a British self-governing territory on the southern tip of the Iberian Peninsula. To formalize the commitment—and confront the habit of women unthinkingly assuming their husbands' surnames—the Beatle formally changed his name to John Winston Ono Lennon.

For their honeymoon, John and Yoko ended up in Room 902 of the Amsterdam Hilton. Everyone was invited to watch.

But there was nothing sexual about this spectacle. For seven days, the duo staged a "bed-in," promoting world peace, resting on the Hilton's fluffy pillows in pajamas as dozens of photographers popped their flashes. John told interviewer Tom Snyder,

> Whatever we did was going to be in the papers. So we decided to utilize the space we would occupy anyway by getting married, with a commercial for peace, and also a theatrical event.... What we had was a seven-day press conference for peace.... Reporters always have five minutes with you or ten minutes with you. We let them ask anything for as long as they wanted for seven days, and all the time, we kept plugging peace.

■ ■ ■

The mood outside the Record Plant was buoyant. As John and Yoko entered the building, everyone on the crowded street—tourists, junkies, hot dog vendors—became enlivened. The excitement was about more than a celebrity sighting. The messages on *Double Fantasy* were reaching people.

In the studio, everyone was having a good time. *Double Fantasy*'s momentum was building. David Geffen's decision to start Geffen Records appeared to be a wise one. John had figured out the special ingredient that "Walking on Thin Ice" needed to push it over the top, a guitar lick based on Sanford Clark's 1956 rockabilly song "The Fool." He walked into the studio, ready to get it done. It was hard to imagine that Julia Lennon had once had to teach her son banjo and ukulele chords to help him become a guitarist. On this particular day, John felt like his playing sounded better than it ever had before.

Brimming with satisfaction, John told his wife, "I think you just cut your first number one, Yoko."

Yoko listened to the track, now mixed with John's guitar work. It was danceable, a club song, but the couple believed they hadn't sold out. This was still a Yoko tune, hopeful but a little unnerving, optimism blended with uncertainty, the themes of eternity and mortality always clashing.

"And when our hearts return to ashes," Yoko sang, "it'll be just a story."

10

Bagism, Shagism, Dragism

This was always a decent neighborhood, even when it was bad."
Officer Peter Cullen had been in the 20th Precinct for sixteen years in 1980, observing the demographic and social shifts on the blocks abutting Central Park with the objectivity his job required, and the subjectivity of a person ingrained in the community. "If I want my uniform cleaned, I'm going to go to my favorite dry cleaner," he said. "If I want Chinese food, I have my favorite Chinese restaurant. If I want Italian food, I know a good Italian restaurant...."

Since 1964, he'd seen landlords abandon buildings, and blocks disintegrate. And he'd watched as some of those properties were gutted and renovated. Gentrification hadn't fully taken root in New York, but it was definitely starting.

"A lot of places didn't change at all," Cullen noted. "We always had a lot of important people on the West Side. Riverside Drive had been nice the whole time. West End Avenue was nice. Central Park West. The lower element lived between those streets, and preyed on the nicer people. That's why we had a lot of work."

Peter was working the 4:00 P.M.-to-midnight shift with Steve Spiro, not his regular partner. On a typical day, he responded to ten to fifteen calls. There were muggings, vehicle accidents, burglaries. Sometimes a person flagged the cops down, saying that an elderly relative needed to get to the hospital.

The diversity of the Upper West Side appealed to Cullen: seeing new faces, meeting people from different countries, having interesting conversations. Other guys bitched about police work. Peter never looked at his watch, wondering when the day would be over. It went by that quickly.

But he never let his guard down, either.

"The more street experience you have, the smarter you get," he said of police work. "Some people never get smart. When you're in a situation, you have to cover your back, cover all of the bases, fill out reports. Politics is as much a part of the job as anything. When you embarrass the New York Police Department, you're taken to task for it."

His cruiser rolled down West Seventy-second Street toward Central Park West. Cullen and Spiro barely glanced at the Dakota. They'd studied the architecture, heard about the history, knew who lived there.

John Lennon may have agitated against authority, but he was a friend of the NYPD. All the cops in the 20th Precinct knew that. The year before, John and Yoko sent a check to the Patrolmen's Benevolent Association (PBA), not to support cops accused of shooting unarmed suspects, but to protect officers who were the victims of gunplay. The $1,000 donation would purchase ten bulletproof vests. The couple also included a note: "The enclosed check expresses our concern for the lives of our police officers in New York City."

As a PBA delegate, Cullen had seen the note himself. To him, the key phrase was "*our* police officers." No one expected John to bow to authority. But in his own community, he respected the job that working guys like Cullen and Spiro had to do.

■　■　■

In June 1968, John and Yoko planned to hold a second bed-in in the United States. But the government invoked a marijuana conviction from the UK to deny Lennon a visa. Undeterred, the couple flew to Montreal, hosting the event in Room 1742 of the Queen Elizabeth Hotel. It was there that the pair introduced the first official single credited to the Plastic Ono Band. This was a far different undertaking than *Two Virgins*. John and Yoko were playing with genuine musicians, most notably Eric Clapton on lead guitar and Klaus Voormann—the conceptual artist the Beatles knew from Hamburg days—on bass. The song, "Give Peace a Chance," became a mighty anthem that some half-million protestors would soon sing at the Washington Monument, at a rally against the Vietnam War.

"Everybody's talking about bagism," John began, mocking trends that distracted from the essential point of working for peace, "shagism, dragism, madism, ragism, tagism, this-ism, ism, ism, ism. / All we are saying is give peace a chance."

As moving as the song may have been, John's fellow Beatles couldn't help but feel discomfort. Everything John did seemed to overshadow them.

The truth was that John felt exhausted by the Beatles—a group he associated with the grind of the earlier days, when they were forced to crank out two albums a year and a single every three months—and rejuvenated by his efforts with Yoko.

He cited "When I'm Sixty-Four" as the type of trite, overly sentimental tune he'd never even listen to on the radio, much less compose himself. The comment was meant as a blatant swipe at Paul, whose cheerful point of view John viewed as shallow. The reality was that John and Paul had spent enough time together for Lennon to recognize his partner's depth. What was true was that Paul had essentially appointed himself head of the Beatles, alienating all of his bandmates because of it. Both Ringo and George—aggrieved that the Beatles only got around to recording his songs years after he wrote them—walked out on sessions, the latter while the cameras were rolling for the *Let It Be* documentary. Not wishing to be bullied or overshadowed by McCartney, George brought in Eric Clapton for assistance on "While My Guitar Gently Weeps."

From Paul's perspective, he had no choice but to place himself in the leadership role. *Someone* had to manage the kindergarten class. George seemed to regard every McCartney suggestion as an assault. And John was treating Paul like Aunt Mimi—that is, searching for ways to defy and provoke him. There was nothing more galling than Yoko's divisive presence in the studio. Unlike other wives and girlfriends, she didn't sit by and watch the boys record, but inserted herself into the proceedings. From her roost on John's amp, the dour-faced Yoko whispered conspiratorially into John's ear, and criticized the music his partners were creating.

At one point, George confronted John about the stressful atmosphere: "What's going on here? You're together all the time. You're freaking me out a bit."

Nobody was happy. John still loved his old friends, but hated George and Paul for their rejection of the Japanese artist.

"I'm for Yoko," John insisted.

The filming of *Let It Be* in 1969 highlighted the ruptures in the group. John suspected that the entire project was being mounted to glorify Paul—with even the cameramen and director conspirators in the plot. McCartney conjectured that John was only interested in performing songs that he'd written. Those who observed the Beatles close up realized that the boys were no longer a band. Instead, the Beatles were composed of four separate individuals veering in different directions, and expecting the others to back them up—like sidemen or session musicians.

■ ■ ■

In the years after December 8, 1980, Mark Chapman would sometimes wonder what might have occurred if he'd landed in New York to discover that John Lennon had suddenly died in a car wreck. Would he have stalked someone else? "I can't answer that question," he told Larry King. "I was so bonded with John Lennon at that point . . . I'd probably be crushed. And at that point, I don't know what I would have done."

What was apparent was that, even in his confused state, his attraction to women was as strong as any of his other impulses.

Here he had a wife in Honolulu—Gloria was a good wife, a sup-
portive wife—but he couldn't contain his animal instincts. The
night before, while sitting alone in his room at the Sheraton, he
began to ponder the fact that he would likely never spend another
evening as a free citizen. Recollecting the story of Holden Caulfield
calling a prostitute to *his* New York hotel, Chapman phoned an
escort service. Remarkably, the woman who turned up was wearing
a green dress, just like the fictitious one in *The Catcher in the Rye*.
She seemed at ease with whatever Chapman wanted, but his head
was cluttered, and his demands were minimal. He fumbled and
groped, but didn't consummate the meeting with intercourse.

Nonetheless, Chapman knew that he had sinned. He and his
wife were Christians, and this was an act of adultery. He just
couldn't control himself. And wasn't that so typical of him? After
working with the Vietnamese refugees, he and his old girlfriend,
Jessica Blankenship, had been heading in the right direction. He'd
registered at her school, Covenant College, an evangelical Presbyterian institution in Lookout Mountain, Tennessee. They studied
together. They prayed together. Things were going great. But there
was something that he hadn't told Jessica. At Fort Chaffee, he'd
fooled around with another girl at a nearby motel. He shouldn't
have, but she'd seduced him, and the memory ate him up. Jessica
was saving herself for marriage; he could have waited, too. She
had no idea he'd done this to her, and he didn't have the courage
to bring it up. But he acted strange. He felt guilty. He couldn't
concentrate. He was neglecting his schoolwork, and eventually
dropped out of college.

Mark later claimed that he'd "wanted to stay in college...I
wanted a career, needed college to do it, couldn't get through
college. And I didn't seek, you know, help from God. I didn't seek
people. I isolated myself...I just kept it all in myself."

Jessica noticed that Mark seemed to cry a lot. There was nothing
wrong with that; she admired people who could express their
emotions. But Chapman would cry over little things, and his

depressive mood lasted for days. Then she discovered that he was spending time that could have been utilized to further his education on the firing range. What was the point of that? She wanted a man with whom she could raise a family. Instead, she found herself with an unpredictable character she feared could hurt himself or someone else. For all the good she'd seen in Mark, she could tell that he was tortured. And it was frightening. Could she really spend the rest of her life with this man?

She decided that she couldn't, and broke off the relationship.

That's where Mark and John Lennon were so similar. Throughout his life, Mark created situations where he felt sad, frustrated, angry—a loser, a nowhere man. He went back to the resettlement camp, but he wasn't the Mark Chapman the administrators had once known. He had a chip on his shoulder. He didn't have patience. And after an argument with the swimming director, he quit.

He took a job as a security guard. Maybe this would be his fresh start. He was smart, and seemed responsible. His bosses liked him and encouraged him to take a week-long weapons course. This was perfect; Mark already knew how to handle guns. The passing grade was sixty. Chapman scored an eighty. Once again, there was opportunity to move forward. He was even offered a promotion. But Chapman said no.

He couldn't handle it.

■　■　■

Paul McCartney was taking on too much. *Magicial Mystery Tour* was the first venture credited to Apple, the Beatles' new company. With the encouragement of gallery owner Robert Fraser, Paul had begun collecting paintings by Belgian surrealist René Magritte, finding particular charm in a self-portrait of the artist holding a green apple in front of his face. This became the symbol of Apple, and Paul spearheaded the corporate effort, as a means for the Beatles to maintain control of their empire. Apple Music oversaw the group's recording and publishing rights. There was also a film division, two retail stores, Apple Management and Apple Electronics—headed by Greek-born Yanni Alexis Mardas, a.k.a. Magic Alex.

When it came to the general concept of Apple, John and Paul stood together. "We're in the happy position of not needing any more money," Paul said at the press conference announcing the company's formation. "So for the first time, the bosses aren't in it for profit. We've already bought all our dreams. We want to share that possibility with others."

John was enamored of the idea of marginalized artists coming to Apple and receiving instant funding. "We want to set up a system where people who just want to make a film about anything, don't have to go on their knees in somebody's office," he stated.

In the electronics arena, John was convinced, Magic Alex exhibited world-changing potential.

Alex first impressed John by creating a "Nothing Box," a small plastic cube with flickering lights. John would stare at the box for hours during acid trips, and seemed impressed with Alex's less than official credentials.

"I'm a rock gardener," he boasted in accented English, "and now I'm doing electronics. Maybe next year I make films or poems. I have no formal training in any of these, but this is irrelevant."

Lennon made sure that Alex was on the company payroll, and guaranteed him ten percent of the profits from his pending inventions. The wunderkind seemed particularly fascinated with paint. He claimed to be developing a type that could make things invisible, and another that would turn a car different colors with the flick of a switch. The Beatles would soon have force fields around their respective homes, he pledged, as well as "wallpaper speakers." Apple subsidized Alex's attempts to devise an artificial sun that could ignite the night sky. When it came time to reveal this novelty, though, Alex claimed that he was still working on finding the proper energy source.

Alex became a regular in the studio, where he'd dissect the technicians' work and complain that what they did was "out of date." George Martin contemplated exiling the interloper, but couldn't because the Beatles appeared so entertained by him.

Alex represented the kinds of problems that occur when people of an artistic persuasion decide to go into business. Because everyone listened to the Beatles by now, Apple's music division was a triumph. But the other branches drained the profits. No one could define exactly what many of the staffers did, other than hang out in the office with friends, talk about abstract ideals, and charge banquets and bar bills to the Beatles.

Something had to be done, and Paul claimed to have a solution. He'd recently married American photographer Linda Eastman, and thought that her father, Lee Eastman, a noted show business attorney, could manage the Beatles. During a meeting, John referred to Eastman as Epstein, the name the family had anglicized. It was a hostile gesture. John's logic: any man who hid his Jewish heritage couldn't be trusted for his transparency in other areas. George and Ringo were equally opposed, viewing Paul's suggestion as a power grab.

John preferred Allen Klein, the former manager of Bobby Darin, Sam Cooke, and the Rolling Stones. Prior to the emergence of Klein, record companies and managers had worked in collusion, often to the detriment of the artist. But Klein went to war with his clients' labels, demanding percentages of profits that he claimed were hidden. Klein said that he was so sure that he could fix Apple that he'd only take a commission of new business. If the company remained in the red, Klein boasted, he'd earn nothing.

Although Lennon was generally wary of fans who tried to insinuate themselves into his life, he allowed Klein to indulge him, quoting lyrics that he knew John had written. John also liked that Klein, unlike the polished Eastman, made no pretense at sophistication. He was a street guy from Newark, New Jersey who never knew his mother—she had died when Allen was a baby—and whose father worked in a butcher shop. John convinced George and Ringo to go with Klein—"he's the only one Yoko liked," John said of the manager choices—but Paul never signed the contract. Who was Yoko to make Beatle decisions? To McCartney, Klein's gangster persona wasn't an act.

Since they were colleagues, Brian Epstein had mentioned Klein periodically to Paul—and Brian hadn't been a fan. Klein had had issues with the Securities and Exchange Commission in the mid-1960s for inflating the stock price of a record company he controlled. And Mick Jagger told McCartney that, after charming the group with his uncouth allure, the manager had hustled away the rights to many of the group's songs. But the other Beatles were so distrustful of Paul by this point that they weren't listening. When Klein renegotiated the group's contract with EMI in 1969, putting the Beatles in position to earn the highest royalties ever bestowed, Klein appeared to be the proper choice.

He also began demanding accountability from Apple employees, cutting unnecessary expense accounts and instituting a time clock. Brian Epstein's loyal lieutenant, Alistair Taylor, was purged to cut ties to the old regime. Apple Electronics was discontinued, as was Magic Alex, who'd sapped the Beatle coffers of some £300,000. John did not rise to his friend's defense. He agreed that there was something poisonous about Alex. In India, Alex was the one who'd stoked the rumors about the Maharishi's sexual proclivities. And within twenty-four hours of Cynthia's separation from John, Alex was next to his friend's estranged wife, plying her with alcohol and saying that she belonged with *him*, not John.

Alex had been an amusing companion, but he'd worn out his welcome. The Beatles had ridden themselves of con men and hangers-on before. At this fragile phase, the Beatles were safer relegating Alex to the past tense than keeping him aboard and letting him steer their ship into the rocks.

■ ■ ■

As others his age were transitioning out of their postadolescence, Mark David Chapman was contemplating the possibilities of acquiring a nuclear device and blowing up a small city. Then he revised his plan. He could hurt a lot more people by murdering someone whom untold millions saw as an idol, a voice, a role model.

"On December 8, 1980, Mark David Chapman was a very confused person," he later explained to Larry King. "He was living inside a paperback novel, J. D. Salinger's *The Catcher in the Rye*. He was vacillating between catching the first taxi home, back to Hawaii, [and] killing...an icon."

In 1977, Chapman visited a public library and studied a map of Hawaii. He returned and looked at it again. When he fantasized about Hawaii, he didn't think about the crime or unemployment rate in Honolulu. He envisioned palm trees and waves and serenity—escape. This was the place where he would calm his anxiety. Mark had just $1,200 in the bank, and hastily withdrew it. He was going to America's fiftieth state.

His money went further than he had anticipated. For nearly a week, he stayed at an upscale hotel, lounged on the beach, and drank at the bar. As his assets dwindled, he transferred to a local YMCA. He was starting to feel better about himself. So he phoned his ex-girlfriend, Jessica.

"Just tell me that you love me," he pleaded.

Jessica didn't like the tone of his voice. She feared that an arbitrary word could start him spiraling in a dangerous direction. Why was he calling her? He had a family. But what if he killed himself? She didn't want to feel responsible for his death.

"Listen, Mark," she began, "why don't you just come home?"

Mark used the remaining funds to fly to Atlanta. It was going to be okay. He imagined himself renewing the romance with Jessica, getting married, having that family she wanted. But once he reached the continent, he realized that she was still scared of him. He was his parents' responsibility now. He returned to their home,

John and Yoko's neighbors were leery when the couple moved into the historic Dakota, on Central Park West, in 1975, but they eventually embraced the pair as part of the community. (© Allan Tannenbaum/SoHo Blues)

The Lennons had recently recorded *Double Fantasy* at the Record Plant. The couple was working on Yoko's single "Walking on Thin Ice" on December 8, 1980. (© Bettmann/Corbis)

In their home office, John left most of the business decisions to Yoko. She expanded their portfolio from music ventures to real estate and cattle. (© Allan Tannenbaum/SoHo Blues)

Paul Goresh was an obsessive fan from New Jersey who once sneaked into the Lennon apartment. Eventually, John grew fond of the photographer, who took one of the last pictures of the former Beatle. (© Bettmann/Corbis)

Record executive David Geffen had been in the studio with the Lennons earlier in the day. Upon hearing of the shooting, he rushed to Roosevelt Hospital to comfort Yoko. (© Allan Tannenbaum/SoHo Blues)

Although Mark David Chapman allegedly shot John Lennon to become a household name, the assassin apparently felt enough embarrassment to cover his face as police led him into the 20th Precinct. (New York Daily News Archive/Getty)

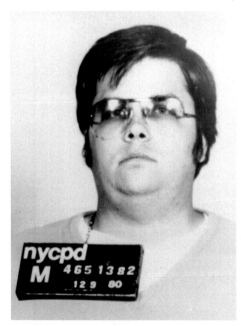

Mark David Chapman's mug shot reveals a nondescript man who'd battled suicidal thoughts and left his wife behind in Hawaii to stalk his former idol in New York. (AFP/Getty)

Ringo Starr and his future wife, actress and model Barbara Bach, rushed to the Dakota from the Bahamas as soon as they learned about the murder. Fans mobbed Ringo outside the building, and he quickly left New York. (© Bettmann/Corbis)

In the days following the killing, fans swarmed the Dakota, singing Lennon songs, lighting candles, and mourning collectively. Approximately 100,000 turned out for a memorial across the street in Central Park. (Keystone/Getty)

In 1980, New York's tabloids still vigorously battled over stories. In this particular photo, mourners appear to show their partiality to the *Daily News*. (© Allan Tannenbaum/SoHo Blues)

12-page pullout on John Lennon—Page 27

DAILY ◉ NEWS

★★★★ 25¢ NEW YORK, WEDNESDAY, DECEMBER 10, 1980 Mostly sunny, windy, 30s. Details p. 73

No Lennon funeral

YOKO: PRAY FOR HIS SOUL

Page 3

EXCLUSIVE!

John Lennon and his accused killer

John Lennon signs autograph for Mark Chapman, his suspected killer, on Monday. PAUL GORESH/DAILY NEWS ©COPYRIGHT 1980 NEW YORK NEWS INC.

Conscious of John's disdain for the "cult of dead celebrity," Yoko opted not to have a funeral. "John loved and prayed for the human race," she said in a statement. "Please do the same for him." (New York Daily News Archive/Getty)

Charge ex-mental patient as killer

Ono: Pray for John's soul; No funeral is scheduled

By ALTON SLAGLE
With Mary Ann Giordano.
D.J. Saunders and Robert Jasinski

His eyes vacant, his hands toying with a tissue, a pudgy, 25-year-old amateur guitar player and former mental patient whom police described as a "wacko" was charged yesterday with the murder of ex-Beatle John Lennon. Lennon's grief-stricken wife, Japanese-born musician Yoko Ono, said there would be no funeral for the gentle man whose music helped define the turbulent, warring '60s and set the world rocking to a new beat.

She asked instead that his friends and millions of fans "pray for his soul." It was not known when or where the 40-year-old musician would be buried.

The assailant, Mark David Chapman of Honolulu, was sent to Bellevue Hospital for psychiatric tests after he admitted: "I killed John Lennon," according to police sources.

THE SOURCES said that when he was asked why he shot Lennon, Chap-

man stared at the ceiling and refused to answer.

Otherwise, during his overnight stay in a cell at the W. 82d St. stationhouse, Chapman was very talkative, freely discussing his background, his Japanese-born wife and Hawaii, according to sources.

But he would not utter a word when questioned about the motive for the slaying except for a cryptic remark about having a "good side and a bad side."

Lennon fell in a hail of bullets Monday night in the entrance to his home, the exclusive Dakota apartments at Central Park West and 72d St., as his wife watched in horror.

The slaying shocked the world.

ACCORDING TO police, Chapman, carrying a snub-nosed pistol and 14 hours of taped Beatles' music in a bag, had haunted the Dakota for three days before pumping four bullets into the peace-loving musician. Lennon was dead within minutes.

With a smirk on his face, Chapman calmly dropped the gun and waited for

See **JOHN** Page 23

John Lennon sings during recording session for his recently released album.

Chapman–A walk in sun to a gun

On the last day he worked, Mark David Chapman signed log as John Lennon, instead of his own name.

By THOMAS HANRAHAN and MARK LIFF

Mark David Chapman, the 25-year-old amateur rock musician held in the murder of John Lennon, signed a security employe logbook in Honolulu with the name "John Lennon" four days before he bought the pistol used in the slaying of the former Beatle.

He also told a fellow employe at the Honolulu condominium complex where he worked as a combination security guard and maintenance man that he was quitting his job and going to London.

"The last day that he worked, he signed 'John Lennon' instead of Mark Chapman to the log," fellow worker Mike Bird said. A check of the log page for that day showed the scrawled "signature" of John Lennon. The signature appeared to be crossed out.

Bird relieved Chapman Oct. 23—the suspect's last day on the job as a guard-maintenance man employed by the Hawaiiana Management Co. at the Waikiki vacation apartments.

POLICE SOURCES ALSO SAID that Chapman, described

See **CHAPMAN** Page 23

IDA LIBBY DENGROVE—NBC—TV VIA AP
Artist sketch of Mark David Chapman

I spoke with suspect hours before

Free-lance photog Paul Goresh.

Paul Goresh, an avid Beatle fan and amateur photographer, first became interested in John Lennon when he heard the Beatles' "Rubber Soul" album in 1966. He was 7 years old.

Today he is 21 and lives in North Arlington, N.J., and has been photographing Lennon the last two years. Here's his story of the events leading to the tragic night at the Dakota, as told to Daily News reporter Larry Sutton:

I arrived at the Dakota about 12:30 p.m. There were already two other people waiting for Lennon. One of them was a tall, husky guy; the other was a blonde girl who appeared to be in her 20s.

About two hours later, Sean Lennon (Lennon's 5-year-old son) arrived home from a two-day vacation with Helen Seamen, his nanny and a nurse. The girl, who claimed to know Helen, approached the child with the man. Sean showed them that he had banged his finger in a door. They talked for several minutes, and then Sean, the nurse and the nanny went inside.

The man then approached me and asked, "Are you waiting for Lennon?" I said that I was.

We started talking. He told me his name was Mark and that he was from Hawaii. He had a Southern accent. I

asked where he got the accent, and he said he was originally from Atlanta. I asked where he was staying while in New York. He indignantly replied: "Why do you want to know?"

I ASKED IF LENNON WAS his favorite musician. He told me no. He said he liked Lennon, but Todd Rundgren was his favorite singer.

Soon, John Lennon, Yoko Ono and several other people came outside. Then Mark approached Lennon with the album. Lennon gladly took it and signed "John Lennon 1980." Then Lennon got into a limo.

We stayed two more hours. Mark kept to himself. I said I was going to leave. He said, "Why don't you wait until they come home? He should be back soon, and you can get your album signed."

I explained I could get it another day.

He said, "I'd wait. You never know if you'll see him again."

I said, "What do you mean? I always see him."

Mark replied, "It's possible he could go to Spain or somewhere tonight, and you'll never get your album signed."

I left shortly after that. Mark stayed. ∎

Daily News, Wednesday, December 10, 1980

The city's tabloids were quick to inform readers of Mark David Chapman's battle with mental illness. The *Daily News* included an interview with Paul Goresh, recounting his conversations with the killer shortly before the shooting. (Daily News Photo Archive/Getty)

Although his musical tastes tended to favor Paul McCartney, New York Mayor Ed Koch and Yoko dedicated Strawberry Fields in John's honor on his birthday, October 9, 1985. (*New York Daily News*)

The centerpiece of Central Park's Strawberry Fields: the "Imagine" mosaic, donated by the city of Naples, Italy, and frequently adorned with flowers by dedicated fans. (Don Emmert/Getty)

but was irritable and accusatory. Clearly, he wasn't welcome under their roof. So he purchased yet another plane ticket and went back to Hawaii.

Seeing no hope, he used the last of his funds to have a good dinner at a steak house. Then he drove a rental car out to a beach on the north shore. If no one wanted him, he wasn't going to burden them any longer. He took a vacuum hose and hooked it to the exhaust pipe, then coiled the device through his window. Turning the ignition key, Chapman closed his eyes and lay back in the driver's seat, waiting for the relief that death would bring.

It didn't happen.

He'd done something wrong.

Chapman was groggy from the fumes when a Japanese fisherman tapped on his window. The plastic hose had melted in the exhaust pipe.

He was so much of a loser that he couldn't even kill himself.

But maybe this was the way it was supposed to happen. The Japanese man wasn't a fisherman at all—he was an angel from God. And God wanted Chapman to live.

He checked himself into the psychiatric unit of Castle Memorial Hospital, under suicide watch. The doctors there liked Chapman. He was intelligent and analytical. The other patients seemed to like him, too. Maybe things weren't that bad. Hawaii was a pretty nice place.

Mark intended to stay there.

■ ■ ■

John had never been comfortable with the MBE he'd received from Queen Elizabeth II. It was an honor he'd been expected to accept in the midst of Beatlemania, when the Fab Four were being depicted as wholesome citizens. But now that he was an outspoken peacenik, he felt like a hypocrite for his affiliation with an empire he held responsible for subjugating people from the Falkland Islands to Northern Ireland. "The bully, that's the establishment," he told ATV. "They know how to beat people up. They know how to gas them, and they have the arms and equipment.... There must be another way."

On November 25, 1969—after retrieving the MBE from the top of Aunt Mimi's television set—he returned the award along with a playful note referring to both Britain's foreign policy and the Plastic Ono Band's latest single:

> Your Majesty,
>
> I am returning this MBE in protest against Britain's involvement in the Nigeria-Biafra thing, against our support of America in Vietnam, and against "Cold Turkey" slipping down the charts.
>
> With Love,
>
> John Lennon

If observers were baffled, they were even more puzzled when John and Yoko cropped their hair—the very symbol of Beatlemania, and the revolution it was said to have engendered—and announced that 1970 was going to be "Year One for Peace." Three months later, the pair asserted that they'd entered a clinic to have his and hers sex change operations. John Lennon was out there, but would he really go this far? The answer was that—his obsession for Yoko, notwithstanding—John still valued his manhood.

The declaration, he quickly conceded, was an April Fools' gag.

For too many years, the press had published every irresponsible rumor they'd heard about John. It was good to get them back once in a while.

■ ■ ■

After being released from Castle Memorial Hospital, Chapman found a job at a gas station and moved in with a Presbyterian minister. But he'd made friends at the hospital, and continued to visit. The other patients looked forward to listening to him play guitar. In his short time in the Aloha State, he'd added a number of Hawaiian songs to his repertoire, and Mark appeared to have the ability to draw out the elderly patients. A few mentioned that he was the first person with whom they'd chatted at length in years. The therapists viewed him as a role model, somebody who'd fought off depression and decided to give of himself to assist others. Mark became a regular volunteer at the facility, then a staffer.

The doctors and nurses all but forgot that this was a man who, until recently, had been possessed by thoughts of suicide and mass murder. They regarded him as a peer and socialized with him after work. Between church and the hospital, he'd once again found acceptance.

While John Lennon was watching his small son grow up, and conceptualizing the songs for *Double Fantasy*, Mark Chapman was rebuilding his self-esteem.

■　■　■

For the first time since 1966, John was back on the concert circuit—only it wasn't with the Beatles. John and Yoko had no qualms about getting on stage to play their music—or to act out Yoko's performance art—but a Beatles tour remained out of the question. Paul was concerned about this; he believed that a band couldn't move forward without testing themselves in front of an audience. In 1969, he suggested that the Beatles appear at venues unannounced, possibly in disguise (he'd eventually have the opportunity to utilize this device, turning up in small, random locations in the early days of Wings). The move would insert energy into the bickering band, Paul reasoned, and keep the public guessing. Ringo supported the concept. George was willing to consider it. As far as Lennon was concerned, Paul might as well have demanded that the band go back to its mop top look and thirty-minute set regimens.

"I'm leaving the group," he informed his bandmates. He described the severance as no different than his divorce from Cynthia.

"I no longer believe in myth," John would elaborate to Jann Wenner, "and Beatles is another myth. I don't believe in it. The dream is over."

If that's what John wanted, Paul said, that's what he'd get. Just as Lennon maintained that the band was at a musical standstill, Paul believed that the group was releasing songs that didn't even sound like Beatles tunes. And it was all because of John persuading everyone else to bring in that insidious Allen Klein. Instead of relying on the steady hand of George Martin, Klein invited erratic American producer Phil Spector to Abbey Road to record the musical accompaniment for the band's last single, "The Long and Winding Road." The diminutive Spector paced around the building like the leader of a fourth-rate dictatorship, acting insane, accompanied by a bodyguard and downing pills. The only Beatle invited to the session was Ringo. At one stage, the orchestra became so exasperated that they walked out. But, according to Paul, Spector lured them back to inflict more harm on the song, adding three trumpets, three trombones, four cellos, and a choir of fourteen women. The entire exercise appeared to be a costly manifestation of everyone else's vexation with Paul.

"No one had asked me what I thought," he told the *Evening Standard*. "I couldn't believe it."

John wasn't the only Beatle who could launch a solo career (in fact, Ringo was also working on an upcoming LP called *Sentimental Journey*). Paul would put out his own album—with *his* wife incorporated into the band—and leave the Beatles, too.

There were reasons, however, that the members agreed to keep this secret from the fans. The Beatles also had an album coming out, *Let It Be*, and Klein didn't want the dissension to undermine his marketing strategy. John agreed not to say anything until the proper time. Then, in April 1970, one month before the release of *Let It Be*, the media received their copies of Paul's premier album, *McCartney*. Included was a series of questions and answers about the project.

In the questionnaire, Paul described his new record as the "start of a solo career," and remarked that he was taking a "break" from the Beatles because of "personal differences, business differences, music differences." He was starting a new company called McCartney Productions, and Allen Klein did not represent him in "any way." While he loved and respected John, Paul said that Lennon's recent music—and related antics—failed to "give me any pleasure." Asked if he could foresee a time when he and John might renew their partnership, Paul flatly answered, "No."

John was irate. He was the one who'd started the Beatles as a teenager in Liverpool, and he was the one who'd broken them up. And he should have been the one, he insisted, to make the announcement. In John's mind, Paul's manufactured question-and-answer session was little more than a cheap gimmick to hype his first solo album—at *Let It Be*'s expense. McCartney countered that, as usual, John was overreacting. The Beatles were already broken up by this point anyway, Paul said. Why continue to lie to the public about it?

On December 31, 1970, Paul took what outsiders considered an extreme step, filing a lawsuit against John, George, and Ringo to dissolve the greatest band the world had ever known.

Paul described the decision as legally necessary, but personally "murderous."

■   ■   ■

Eight years after the Beatles' split, Mark David Chapman was sitting in a Honolulu movie theater, watching the 1956 adaptation of the Jules Verne novel *Around the World in 80 Days*, when his heart lifted. There was so much of the world he hadn't seen, and—like Phileas Fogg, the film's main character—Mark would now embark on an international journey. Within days, he had the trip charted out: the People's Republic of China—newly opened to western travel—Japan and South Korea, picturesque Switzerland, the ancient civilization of Iran. In the Holy Land, Mark could stand in the Garden of Gethsemane, follow Jesus' final walk down Via Dolorosa, touch the Stone of the Anointing, where the Savior's body was prepared for burial, and then marvel at the tomb from which he rose again to give mankind everlasting life.

Chapman borrowed the funds from the hospital's credit union and was granted a six-week leave of absence. Old associates from the YMCA offered free or inexpensive accommodations. The trip was complicated and had numerous revisions, and Mark frequently found himself on the phone with a helpful travel agent named Gloria Abe. As he trekked about the globe, his thoughts often returned to the kind Japanese-American woman. After stopping off in Georgia to visit his parents, Mark flew back into Honolulu, seemingly invigorated. He invited Gloria to his church, and the Buddhist woman converted to Christianity. In January 1979, the two were walking down the beach when Mark came to a sudden halt. Gloria watched him painstakingly scribble in the sand: "Will you marry me?"

Gloria bent down next to him and wrote, "Yes."

It was all coming together. Chapman and Gloria hugged, and she hopped on his back as he trotted along the water. It was a scene as romantic as Mark had ever imagined.

He and his Japanese bride-to-be.

A vista from a John and Yoko song.

11

WALKING SHELL

It's a pity," Paul McCartney told *Life* magazine in 1971. "I like fairy tales. I'd love it to have had the Beatles go up in a little cloud of smoke, and the four of us just find ourselves in magic robes, each holding an envelope with our stuff in it. But you realize that you're in real life."

One day, he predicted, his fondness for his former bandmates would return. "But at the moment," he added, "I'm not stuck on them."

This was apparent when Paul and wife Linda released the album *Ram* in 1971. In his song "Too Many People," McCartney took a swipe at John's pedantry, crooning, "Too many people preaching practices." Observers wondered if he was also referring to John with the line "You took your lucky break and broke it in two."

John fired his own volleys at McCartney with "How Do You Sleep?" The tune blatantly implied that Paul's crowning glory was the song "Yesterday" and that he "lived with the straights," basking in their breathless praise. Even as Lennon's critics alleged that Yoko had some Svengali-like hold on him, John jabbed at Paul's inability to stand up to Linda, characterizing McCartney as a man who'd "jump when your momma tell you anything."

And if that wasn't enough, "The sound you make is muzak to my ears / You must have learned something in all those years."

Paul was accustomed to John's barbs. The two had been bashing each other—good-naturedly and otherwise—since they were teens. But what angered McCartney about "How Do You Sleep?" were reports that Yoko had helped her husband conjure up the lyrics. And if Paul had any doubts as to where the other Beatles stood, the tune featured George Harrison on slide guitar.

Still, George gained his true revenge when his song "My Sweet Lord"—from *All Things Must Pass*, the triple album of tunes he'd been stockpiling since 1966—became the first #1 single by an ex-Beatle. A year later, in 1971, he organized a concert for famine victims in Bangladesh—the prototype for charity concerts like Live 8 and Hope for Haiti—featuring George on stage alongside heavyweights like Eric Clapton, Bob Dylan, Billy Preston, Leon Russell, and Ringo.

Paul acknowledged his former companion's achievements with a decided aloofness. "I think George has shown recently that he was no dummy," McCartney said in *Life*.

As always, Ringo managed to navigate the path between the warring Beatles most adeptly, drumming on the *Plastic Ono Band* album and on *All Things Must Pass*. His 1973 album, *Ringo*, featured contributions by all three of his former bandmates. The LP went platinum and hit #2 on the *Billboard* charts. John, Paul, and George would pool their talents again on Ringo's 1974 album, *Goodnight Vienna*.

"I'm most happy, I think we all are in a way...for Ringo's success," John told Tom Snyder. "He wasn't known for writing his own material, and there was a bit of a worry.... How is his recording career going to be?' In general, it's probably better than mine."

■　■　■

At the Record Plant, label impresario David Geffen noticed the satisfaction on John's face as he and Yoko listened to "Walking on Thin Ice." Lennon was back in the middle of the entertainment business, but he felt like he was manning the controls. He and Yoko had been artistic partners now for well over a decade. Before anyone realized it, their time as a duo eclipsed that of the Beatles.

John and Geffen discussed the marketing progress of *Double Fantasy*. It was on the verge of hitting #1 in the UK, and John couldn't wait. The entire studio process appeared enjoyable to him. There was none of the creepy murmuring that John and Yoko had shared during the *Let It Be* sessions. Now the two smiled at the technicians and each other. As always, John laughed with producer Jack Douglas.

No one was really keeping track of the hours. Time was moving quickly, always the sign of a successful project. Geffen and John made plans to have dinner the next night.

■   ■   ■

John never regretted his decision to not play at Woodstock. Organizers had wanted a Beatles appearance, but John had insisted that the Plastic Ono Band also perform. At the time, the demand seemed excessive, and John stayed home.

As he'd said before, "I'm for Yoko."

Nonetheless, John took partial credit for creating the concepts inspiring those who converged on Woodstock—the largest gathering, he remarked, for something other than a war—and took this as a positive view of the future. "This is only the beginning," he told ATV. "The sixties bit was just a sniff. The sixties was just waking up in the morning, and we haven't even got to dinner time yet. And I can't wait, you know. I just can't wait. I'm so glad to be around."

Four months after Woodstock, John and Yoko resumed their spots at the head of the peace movement, renting billboards in New York, Los Angeles, London, Amsterdam, Paris, Rome, Athens, West Berlin, Toronto, Hong Kong, and Tokyo, proclaiming,

WAR IS OVER (If You Want It).

Happy Christmas from John and Yoko.

In 1971, the couple followed up this statement with the song "Happy Xmas (War Is Over)." Like *Double Fantasy* would be, it was recorded at the Record Plant. Producer Phil Spector invited the Harlem Community Choir into the studio to sing background, adding to both the holiday flavor and the overall theatrics of the tune.

It's a theme that the years and the turns in John's life wouldn't dim. "We're carrying the torch," he'd tell *Rolling Stone*, "like the Olympic torch, passing it from hand to hand, to each other, to each country, to each generation."

At times, it felt as if every song was an exercise in some type of self-help—at the very beginning of the song, Yoko could barely be heard whispering, "Happy Christmas, Kyoko," followed by John softly continuing, "Happy Christmas, Julian." In 1970, John had spent four months with Dr. Arthur Janov, architect of a discipline called primal therapy. Janov urged Lennon to relive his most painful memories, then release his combusted emotions with a piercing "primal scream." Perhaps the most mesmeric corollary of this process was the song "Mother"—in which John cried for both Alf and Julia Lennon: "Mama don't gooo-oooo / Daddy come home."

Lenny Kravitz would later call the song "one of the most hard-core pieces of music ever recorded."

But Yoko would soon endure an anguish more pronounced than the absenteeism of John's parents. In 1971, Yoko's ex-husband, Tony Cox—who'd joined an insular religious group called Church of the Living Word—vanished with Kyoko, moving her from continent to continent, ahead of the investigators hired by the Lennons. Yoko wouldn't hear from her daughter again until 1998. Both she and John would later cling to the little family they had.

■   ■   ■

Mark David Chapman and his wife, Gloria, moved into a condominium in the Diamond Head Tower at Kukui Plaza in downtown Honolulu. In order to earn a few extra dollars, Mark took a job in Castle Memorial Hospital's print shop, cutting himself off from the therapeutic atmosphere that seemed to benefit him. Now Mark no longer saw the patients or staffers he regarded as friends. He worked in solitude, alone with his thoughts.

The irritability he'd previously displayed asserted itself again. He became embroiled in the politics of his wife's job at the travel agency, arguing with her boss and forcing her to quit. Without the protection of the doctors who knew his history, Chapman's anti-social traits became a liability in the print shop. He was fired at one point, then rehired. But he saw enemies everywhere, and resigned after getting into a loud altercation with a nurse.

Once again, he took a security job, this time at a luxury building. He justified the move by claiming that he'd be better off because he could interact with people again. But Mark David Chapman had turned a corner. Instead of seeking the companionship of Christians who could engage his mind in Bible study courses and persuade him to bring his guitar to ecumenical events, he began drinking alone.

His mind bounced back and forth. He purged his record collection—selling or throwing away his evil rock 'n' roll albums—then regretted it and began going to music stores to find replacement albums. Once he'd replenished his archives, he sold the records again, and violently destroyed his turntable. Just as he'd once turned Gloria on to Christianity, he now ordered her to read *The Catcher in the Rye*. He wrote the Hawaii attorney general, inquiring about the logistics of changing his name to Holden Caulfield.

"Mark David Chapman at that point was a walking shell who didn't ever learn how to let out his feelings of anger, of rage, of disappointment," he'd tell Larry King, speaking of himself in the third person. "I believe I was schizophrenic at the time."

■   ■   ■

As Chapman struggled with mental illness, the phantom of the Beatles continued to haunt John. "I've gotten used to the fact, just about, that whatever I do is going to be compared to the other

Beatles," he told *Rolling Stone*. "If I took up ballet dancing, my ballet dancing would be compared with Paul's bowling."

But he was adamant that the Beatles would never re-form, equating the decision with that of a Ph.D. candidate returning to high school. The whole purpose of the Beatles, at least in the later years, had been encouraging young people to think for themselves. Why should all four Beatle members now surrender their instincts to satisfy society?

Besides, John stated, his post-Beatles music was better.

The mean-spirited "How Do You Sleep" notwithstanding, John's 1971 *Imagine* album stood at the same level as the year's bounty of stellar offerings—*Led Zeppelin (IV)*, *Who's Next*, the Rolling Stones' *Sticky Fingers*, Elton John's *Madman Across the Water*, Jethro Tull's *Aqualung*, David Bowie's *Hunky Dory*, and Cat Stevens' *Teaser and the Firecat*, to name a few—overshadowing Paul McCartney's *Ram*. The title track would never lose its relevance, and other songs—"Crippled Inside," "Jealous Guy," and "Give Me Some Truth"—conveyed raw honesty from deep within John's soul. In what may have been rock's most fruitful year, *Imagine* was as fine as anything pressed onto vinyl.

"Those Plastic Ono Band songs stand up to any song that was written when I was a Beatle," John told *Playboy*. "Now, it may take you twenty or thirty years to appreciate that, but the fact is, if you check those songs out, you will see that it is as good as any fucking stuff that was ever done."

What John found most liberating was the fact that he wasn't shackled to a particular group of musicians. "I can change musicians whenever I like," he told Tom Snyder. "If you play with the same person all the time, it just gets into a rut. Even if you play tennis with the same person...it just comes to the time that you know every move, and you have to find somebody else to play with."

John even varied the name of the group from time to time, calling his combo the Plastic Ono Nuclear Band, the Plastic UFO Ono Band, and, when performing with fellow avant-garde activist Frank Zappa, the Plastic Ono Mothers.

■ ■ ■

In the fall of 1980, Chapman believed he'd "dug a big hole" for himself. And, for some reason, he blamed John Lennon for his frame of mind.

"I was sitting in my apartment and I opened a Beatle album, a *Sgt. Pepper's* album," he'd later testify, "which has all four of them in it, large photographs of them. And earlier, I had checked out some books from the library about John Lennon...and some of the things I'd seen in the books had angered me."

One of Chapman's objections centered on a photo of John at the Dakota. It wasn't fair that Chapman was eking out a living as a security guard when the ex-Beatle went home each night to a "ritzy building."

It was infuriating. Something had to be done.

Said Chapman,

> It was more about me and not him. I was probably mad at myself for my failures. So, I am looking at this album, back at the apartment. I just saw his face, and it seemed like it all came together—the solution to my problem of being confused and feeling like a nobody. And I said, "Wouldn't it be something if I killed this individual?"

Chapman applied for a pistol permit, claiming that his home had been burglarized over the summer. The Honolulu Police Department did a criminal background check. His record was clean.

The permit was granted.

The little people returned. They knew what he'd been thinking, and begged him to reconsider. He couldn't do something so destructive, they told him. Not only would he ruin his life, but he would hurt Gloria in ways she didn't deserve.

But Mark was the leader of the little people. He controlled them. They didn't control him. And even though they were right, the other voices he heard were stronger. On October 20, he read an article in the Honolulu *Star Bulletin* about *Double Fantasy*. There was a quote from John about his guilt over earning his fortune—and his reflection that maybe some of his radical posturing had been less than sincere.

This was the confirmation Chapman needed. He was going to New York.

Three days later, he quit his job. Instead of signing out with the usual nickname of "Chappy," he wrote "John Lennon." He peered at the words, then had a change of heart and crossed the name out.

Gloria's father lent Mark $5,000. He used $169 to purchase the five-shot, short-barrelled .38. The salesman was helpful and gracious—Japanese-American, like Gloria.

His last name was Ono.

Two days later—on October 29—Mark had the gun in his pocket while he camped out in front of the Dakota, studying its moldings, admiring its importance. All he needed were bullets. When he phoned a gun dealer, though, the man chuckled.

"You're not from around here, are you?"

Chapman had to come up with an alternative plan, and boarded a flight for Georgia. Without calling beforehand, he turned up at the home of his ex-girlfriend, Jessica Blankenship. Jessica had told her parents about Mark's perennial battle with mental illness, and they were less than happy to see him. Chapman and Jessica had a short, strained conversation. Then he left.

He had a goal to fulfill.

"I need a favor," he told a friend from his days at Fort Chaffee. "I'm going to New York City, and I want a gun to protect myself. Do you have any bullets?"

"What kind do you need?"

"Something with real stopping power."

They settled for five cartridges of the hollow-point variety—the type that expand as they blast through a body. Chapman repaired to the woods, practicing his aim.

He was pretty good.

■ ■ ■

Ellen Chesler, the chief of staff for City Council President Carol Bellamy, arrived home to the Dakota at 7:30 P.M., heartened to see the old building, framed so brilliantly by Central Park and the dark December sky.

Many of the families in the building had finished dinner already, and Ellen could hear the voices of children playing in the Dakota's large hallways. Even though she couldn't count each adult in the building as an intimate, she probably knew the name of every kid. Sean Lennon seemed to be around often, telling stories and smiling. Like everyone else, Ellen had been reading the interviews related to *Double Fantasy*, and John and Yoko's quotes about family life. Because she dealt with politicians all day, she looked at every public statement with a pinch of cynicism. But when it came to Sean, the Lennons were telling the truth. He was a polite, happy kid, and they worked hard to make his life as normal as possible.

The children his age were too young to understand the enormity of the Beatles. They saw John a lot, and knew him as Sean's good-humored, attentive father.

Ellen entered her apartment, then picked up her baby daughter. Her mind flashed briefly to that pudgy guy with the Southern accent she'd seen outside the building—the same guy who'd been hanging around the Dakota since the weekend. Other neighbors had apparently noticed him, too.

"There had been some concern about him, just because he was around so much," Ellen remembered. "You'd look and say, 'Oh boy, that guy's here again.' But he was behaved, and seemed normal like a lot of other fans."

For Ellen Chesler, there were bigger issues than a John Lennon devotee who seemed to have a little too much time to himself. Tomorrow, the grind at City Hall would start all over again: fiscal issues, labor strife, welfare, the rebuilding of the South Bronx.

"We dealt with so many things," she said.

■ ■ ■

John didn't always like the way his activism impacted his work. "It almost ruined it," he related to *Rolling Stone*. "It became journalism and not poetry."

Yet, with the pressure of being a Beatle removed, John felt that he had so much to say. The song "Imagine" hit a nerve with both supporters and detractors, who found the notions of no war—that is, no defense spending—and no religion threatening. The resistance to these messages raged for years, but John didn't back down as he had done after the "more popular than Jesus" remarks. There was no Brian Epstein around to convince him to play nice. Earlier in 1971, he'd released the single "Power to the People," an angrier, more militant version of "Give Peace a Chance": "Say we want a revolution / We better get it on right away."

The new members of his social network—self-styled radicals in both the UK and the United States—stoked John's aggressive political outlook. There was a presidential election coming up in 1972, and some Lennon associates believed he'd be the perfect vehicle for forcing Richard Nixon out of office. Plans were made for a tour that would combine music with speeches against the Vietnam War. For the first time, eighteen-year-olds could vote in a presidential campaign, and the power brokers in Washington began watching Lennon closely. In December 1971, he headlined at the Chrysler Arena in Ann Arbor, Michigan, agitating for the release of John Sinclair, a left-wing activist sentenced to ten years in prison for possession of two joints of marijuana.

Two days later, Sinclair was released.

What John may not have realized was that the U.S. government had undercover agents planted in the audience, transmitting every word the singer uttered back to Washington. With the election less than a year away, the decision was made to stop John Lennon.

■ ■ ■

In 1968, John and Yoko had been in Ringo Starr's central London apartment when police raided, busting the pair for cannabis possession and for obstructing the officers executing the search warrant. Fearing a protracted legal battle, and Yoko's deportation back to Japan, John tried to make the case go away by pleading guilty to a misdemeanor charge and paying a fine of £150.

But the conviction would follow him to the United States as John and Yoko began establishing roots in New York City. Initially, the pair had journeyed across the Atlantic to search for Yoko's daughter, Kyoko. But over time, they fell in love with the city's energy and possibility; John compared it to Rome, circa the first century. "I should have been born in New York," John told *Rolling Stone*. "I should have been born in the Village. That's where I belong. . . . That's why I'm here now. I'm here just to breathe it."

Then, suddenly, in 1972, shortly before the presidential election, John and Yoko were served with deportation orders. The Nixon administration contended that the procedure was commonplace; immigration laws at the time barred anyone with a drug conviction—no matter how minimal—from the United States. But John had the sense that his phone was being tapped, and someone was following him. Still, because he was paranoid by nature, he wasn't really sure.

The Lennons' lawyer appealed the directive, slowing the deportation process. With each newspaper article on the case, the number of Lennon advocates expanded, transcending the predictable network of long-hairs and lefties. "This was really an unforgivable attack on John Lennon," recalled Edward Morrision, the city's deputy mayor at the time. "There were very few merits to the administration's case. Everything was being done on a political basis.

"It was dreadful, just dreadful."

Morrison waded into the storm after Mayor John V. Lindsay professed that Lennon was a "cultural asset" to the city. But John was uncertain about how far the words would resonate.

"John had a lot of anxiety about this, no question about it," Morrison remembered, "as did Yoko. They really didn't want to leave New York. I think the city exemplified to him freedom, a place where he could really pursue his range of interests. He felt a great deal of compatibility with people he'd gotten to know in the city, and others he was looking forward to meeting."

For all the faults of its government, John had also developed a warmth for the United States. "This is where the music came from," he told Tom Snyder. "This is what influenced my whole life, and got me where I am today, as it were. And I love the place.... 'The Statue of Liberty. Welcome.' I even brought my own cash."

As Morrison—chairman of the now-defunct Manhattan Liberal Party—advised John of his options, the two formed a friendship. The Morrison family's four sons all lived at home at the time, and John occasionally showed up at their West Eighty-sixth Street apartment with presents for the kids.

On rare occasions, John mentioned his own son, and how much he missed Julian.

"For the most part, I think he enjoyed, once in a while, being in the company of somebody who was totally straight," Morrison said. "There were so many people asking him for things, looking for some material piece that he could deliver, and my wife and I didn't want any of that. We were there to help him. And I think that was something novel."

It was Morrison who introduced Lennon to another supporter, a liberal congressman from Greenwich Village named Ed Koch. The thought of the scraggly Beatle huddling with the blunt, high-strung future mayor is an amusing one. But Koch maintained that it was relatively uneventful.

"I don't want you to think we planned our next march," says Koch. "He was the epitome of decorum. He was a little schoolboy."

The congressman introduced a bill allowing the Attorney General to waive the exclusion of immigrants previously convicted of marijuana charges. "It did not have any impact," Koch said. "It was never passed. But it brought notoriety and attention to the case."

Eventually, John countersued the U.S. government, and, on October 7, 1975—some five months after the Vietnam War officially ended, and slightly more than a year after Nixon abdicated in disgrace—the New York State Supreme Court reversed the deportation order. On July 7, 1976, John finally received his green card, crowing to the press, "It's good to be legal again."

In four years, the Washington establishment had accepted the New York view that Lennon's talents benefited the nation—so much so that, when President Jimmy Carter was inaugurated, John was invited to the festivities.

■　■　■

After scoring some ammo for his .38 in Georgia, Chapman returned to New York, where he took time away from lurking outside the Dakota to go to the movies. He selected *Ordinary People*, about a suicidal, upper-middle-class teen returning home after a stay in a psychiatric hospital. The film apparently hit a nerve in Chapman, and he phoned his wife.

Honks honked and buses rumbled as Chapman stood on a Manhattan street, whispering into the pay phone. "I came here to kill John Lennon," he admitted, his eyes darting to ensure that his secret was safe from passersby.

"Come home," Gloria beseeched her husband. "Come home."

"I *will* come home," he agreed, his voice choked with emotion. "I'm not going to do this. This is a great victory. Your love has saved me, Gloria."

Chapman boarded a plane to Honolulu. Gloria was waiting in the condominium. As soon as Mark passed through the door, she embraced him, begging him to see the good he already had in his life. His body—chilled for so many days on Central Park West—felt soothed by the tropical air. The smell of salt water wafted through the window. Chapman promised to take control of his mental health. To pacify his wife, he made an appointment with a clinical psychologist.

He never kept it.

"The emotions started building again," he'd testify. "It was a compulsion. I guess somebody like me—at the time feeling like a nobody—gets a hold of something like that, it is very hard to let go. . . . It is very hard to stop it, if nothing changes at the time dramatically.

"And nothing did change very much."

Chapman chose to return to New York. But he knew that Gloria wouldn't approve of his reasons. So he lied. "I'm going to find myself," he asserted. "I'm going to write a book, a kid's book, and just try to get my life together."

Gloria wanted to believe her husband, and gave him her blessing. But her doubts weighed her down. On December 6, she walked him to the gate in the airport, weeping as he boarded the plane with his gun in his suitcase. He remembered those cries all the way across the Pacific and then, the American continent. In New York, he slipped into a taxi and asked the driver if he wanted a hit of cocaine.

■　■　■

Nineteen-year-old Adam Shanker completed his bartending shift at the Knickerbocker Pub on East Forty-ninth Street, and began walking down Madison Avenue, a copy of *Playboy* magazine rolled up under his arm. The cover featured a photo of Ringo's girlfriend, Barbara Bach, against a backdrop of mist, blackness, and faux stars, a nipple protruding against the sheer fabric wrapped around her figure. Inside were interviews with football coach Bum Phillips, author Stephen King, and John and Yoko.

Men always joked that they purchased *Playboy* for the articles, but in this case, Adam really had. He'd grown up as a Beatles fan, singing *Dizzy Miss Lizzy* and *Long Tall Sally* into his hairbrush.

Since then he had bought the original vinyl pressings of every Beatles album released in the United States—in both mono and stereo. In the ten years since the group had split up, he'd continued to support all four members, filling his bedroom with *Thirty Three & 1/3* by George Harrison, *Ringo the 4th*, *Venus and Mars* by Paul McCartney and Wings, and now *Double Fantasy*.

"The new LP was great," Adam said. "Yoko's songs were great, too. It was a time when a lot of artists who'd made their mark in the sixties and seventies didn't know what to do in the eighties. But *Double Fantasy* was fresh. There was an excitement that John Lennon was back."

At Forty-eighth Street, Adam turned right, moving toward the crowds at Rockefeller Center, gathered for the annual lighting of the Christmas tree. He wondered if John would show up one night at some small venue in the New York and play a set. How could he find out about that?

Everyone at Rockefeller Center seemed happy. The air was crisp; winter was coming. The red and green bulbs on the upper branches of the Norway spruce twinkled and glowed. Adam didn't celebrate Christmas, but the scene made him optimistic about the coming year. He stood there, observing, then started back toward Grand Central Station to get the train home to New Rochelle.

He planned to find a quiet seat and finish the *Playboy* interview with John and Yoko. Then he'd listen to *Double Fantasy* again before going to sleep.

■ ■ ■

The sounds in the next room infuriated Chapman, and it wasn't the first time, either. That's what you got for $16.50 a night at the YMCA—two gays, next door, fucking. This was supposed to be the Young Men's *Christian* Association, and here were these sodomites, sinning with impunity. Chapman had his gun and his bullets now. Maybe *this* was why the hand of God had brought him here. He could kick in the door, and blow those fags away.

But who'd care? Who'd remember? It wasn't worth it. He'd save his ammo for John Lennon.

Chapman couldn't stay at the Y anymore. The next day he checked into the Sheraton. When he got to his room he pulled an album from his suitcase and studied it. *The Ballad of Todd Rundgren*. Like Chapman, Todd had been a Beatles fan. But now he knew what Lennon really was. It couldn't be clearer than in the 1973 song "Rock and Roll Pussy": "Will you, will you, get your nails dirty / Or are you only just a rock and roll pussy?"

This was why Rundgren was now Chapman's favorite singer. He said what no one else wanted to admit about Lennon. He and John had even had a feud in *Melody Maker*. Todd said Lennon was a phony who took up causes to seek attention. "I never claimed to be a revolutionary," John replied in a letter to the magazine. "But I am allowed to sing anything I want! Right?"

Now Chapman was going to stand up to John as well. Prior to his departure for the Dakota on December 8, he'd leave the Rundgren album on the shrine he had built on top of his dresser at the Sheraton, along with a Bible, a letter of praise from his supervisors in Fort Chaffee, and a *Wizard of Oz* poster he'd bought between shifts outside Lennon's front door.

■ ■ ■

Before starting the midnight-to-8:00 A.M. "lobster shift" at the New York *Daily News*, reporter Paul LaRosa took his younger brother and sister to the Christmas tree lighting, finding a parking space just blocks from Rockefeller Center. Even in the busiest part of the city, LaRosa could always unearth a spot. It came from being a lifelong New Yorker whose job required him to get in and out of the city's myriad of neighborhoods quickly, like a member of some tactical squad.

LaRosa had been born in East Harlem, then raised at the Monroe Houses in the Bronx. At the Blessed Sacrament School, he was one year ahead of future Supreme Court Justice Sonia

Sotomayor. He'd always wanted to be a reporter, chronicling the city's ever-growing history in black and white for the masses riding in on the 7 train from Queens or the A line from Washington Heights. When he was a senior at Fordham University, he took a job at WPIX, a local television station in the same building as the *News*. The plan was to maneuver his way over to the newspaper. When a copy boy position opened at the tabloid, Paul grabbed it.

In 1975, the copy boys sat on a wooden bench, waiting to be summoned by reporters typing their stories one page at a time. When a page was completed, it was held in the air, and the reporter would shout, "Copy!" The task for LaRosa and his peers was getting the copy to an editor quickly, as well as fetching coffee for the writers and, when the situation warranted, a gift for someone's wife.

Copy boys were expected to ascend quickly, and Paul followed the pattern, becoming a caption writer, assistant on the city desk, and finally a reporter. Although he lived in Bayside, Queens, far from the center of midtown, he tried to understand the dynamics of both the glamour and low-rent precincts of the city, and—like so many others—had witnessed the sight of John and Yoko strolling, arm in arm, by the Dakota.

As with everyone his age, he loved the Beatles. "Once they came roaring into your life," he noted, "you could never look back."

But, although LaRosa valued John's work as a singles performer, McCartney was the member to whom he best related. "It's probably because of my name," he said. "I'd always been more of a Paul guy."

■ ■ ■

Producer Jack Douglas walked John and Yoko to the elevator at the Record Plant. While John and Douglas discussed their recording schedule for the next day, Yoko stifled a yawn. But she wasn't bored. She was a little tired—but happy.

The pair stepped onto the lift, and John turned around.

"See you at nine o'clock tomorrow," Jack said, watching the doors close on John's smiling face.

12

TOOT AND SNORE

In the limo, Yoko turned to John: "You want to go somewhere for dinner?"

John shook his head. "Let's go home," he answered. "I want to be with Sean."

John's attachment to his son was stronger than anything he'd ever experienced. As intense as the relationship was with Yoko, it was as conditional as any other male-female union. Of course, he'd grown up with two maternal figures fighting over him. But because John had never fully belonged to either Julia or Mimi, he was left with an emotional deficit that only Sean had been able to fill.

Not only did John see much of himself in Sean, he also saw aspects of Julian. Away from the carousel of the music business, John missed those years away from Julian, and was working to repair the link. But it wasn't going to come easy. Julian was a strong-willed young man who wouldn't ignore the way his famous father had wounded him.

In 1999, Julian told the *Austin Chronicle* that he was "surprised" that John hadn't attempted to re-establish their closeness until Sean came into his life: "It was only then that it started clicking— 'Maybe I should try to make it up to my son who I've not paid attention to for... almost twenty years.' And for me, that's very disturbing. It saddens me. It saddens me a great deal."

John was repentant. And unlike his own father, Alf, he acted out of love, not opportunism.

In 1964, while the Beatles were filming *A Hard Day's Night*, Alf Lennon suddenly materialized in Brian Epstein's office, his greasy hair slicked back over a balding pate. "I'm John Lennon's father," he announced to the receptionist as an accompanying reporter scribbled notes.

The image-conscious Epstein appeared alarmed and interrupted the Beatles on set. Throughout his life, John had contemplated the circumstances under which he'd again see his father. But the fantasy had never involved Brian Epstein and a member of the British press. Nonetheless, on Epstein's orders, John was soon in a car, motoring to his manager's office.

Alf warmly extended a hand to his abandoned child. John wouldn't shake it. Glancing sideways at the reporter, Alf declared, "You can't turn your back on your family."

Unimpressed, John told his father to leave.

Epstein didn't want this type of publicity, and called the reporter's publisher. A deal was cut. In exchange for a series of exclusives with the Beatles, the paper would kill the dismal tale of John's paternity.

Alf refused to disappear, courting the press until the *Daily Express* took the risk of alienating Epstein by running a story on John's long-lost father. Not long afterward, Alf boldly knocked on John's door. Cynthia greeted him, and immediately noticed the resemblance. This time Alf was invited inside. Over cheese on toast, he told Cynthia about making money and losing money. He was never afraid of work, he stressed. In fact, he was currently employed as a dishwasher at a hotel just a few miles away.

John's anger dissipated, at least temporarily. Yes, he understood Alf's motivations—he was in the music business, after all, and knew a lot of shysters—but John was also grateful to have his father back.

A year later John was mortified to discover that Alf had launched his own recording career. His single, "That's My Life (My Love and My Home)," was being released on New Year's Eve. John asked Epstein if something could be done to sabotage the effort. What if Alf's song became so popular that it distracted from the Beatles' string of hits?

"I don't think we have to worry about that," Epstein replied.

Displaying little of his son's musical prowess, Alf essentially talked through a nicotine-stained variation of "My Way," telling listeners about the trials of his seafaring choices: "Pity was my partner, all along / Yet, listen to me…now, I've grown strong."

The song was all but ignored. In 1966, Alf tried again, releasing three more singles under the name Freddie Lennon. While he never cracked the Beatles' social network, he did manage to ingratiate himself with a number of rock 'n' roll fans, particularly an eighteen-year-old Rolling Stones supporter named Pauline Jones. After the pair eloped in 1966, John once again extended himself, making peace with this odd couple. Pauline was given a job both watching Julian and organizing the Beatle's fan mail. The singer also purchased the couple a house in Brighton, where John's half-brothers, David Henry and Robin Francis Lennon, were born. With his new family to occupy him, Alf drifted apart from John.

Still, during John's primal therapy phase, he was possessed by a great need to see Alf. When the senior Lennon showed up at his son's house, a crying John shrieked at his father about his abandonment and the opportune timing of his return. John then ordered Alf never to contact him again.

This time, the rupture lasted until Sean was a year old, and John learned that his father was dying of stomach cancer. The former Beatle phoned Alf from the Dakota, apologizing for the screaming session, and sent a large bouquet of flowers to the hospital. Nonetheless, when John later offered to pay for his father's funeral, Pauline rejected the overture.

As with Julian, there was much about the relationship that remained unresolved.

■　■　■

Ken Dashow carefully scaled the stairs to the midtown roof, holding the soggy bag of freshly poured hot chocolates to his winter coat.

It was one of the rare moments when he wasn't near a radio.

Ken had helped build his four-watt high school radio station, at Poly Prep in Brooklyn, then worked his way onto the air at Hobart College, on the northern end of Seneca Lake, in the Finger Lakes region of upstate New York. From the start, he'd received positive feedback, and by the spring he'd begun to wonder whether a guy like him really belonged in a place nicknamed "the lake trout capital of the world." When his sophomore year started, Ken was back in the city, at NYU.

Although he found himself among dozens of aspiring deejays, Ken decided not to join NYU's storied radio station. Instead, he sent his Hobart tapes out to stations around the metro area.

That's how he got his first paying radio gig, at a country station in Newton, New Jersey. Ken knew nothing about the genre—he was a rock 'n' roll guy—but the people listening to nineteen-year-old "Cousin Ken" never would have guessed.

In 1980, he was still paying his dues. Every weekend, he drove out to WRCN FM in Riverhead, Long Island. The station was located seventy-five miles from the center of the city, but Ken could play all the classic rock he wanted. To him, the Beatles were responsible for

> the greatest rhythms, the most infectious musical hooks ever created. Some people get to touch the muse once in a blue moon, and it occasionally passes near them. Paul had a 3,000-watt line into the muse that just gave him riff after riff, and poetic line after line. And John was such a perfect partner for Paul's fun, poppy whimsy. He provided that cynical view of the world, a depth, an intimacy. They didn't always agree, but everyone else agreed they wrote great songs. When I got older, as opposed to saying, "Well, that was fun for an early pop phase," I had a better understanding of how they changed the world.

Ken's big break wouldn't come until 1982, when he was hired by WAPP, "The Apple," with its giant transmitter on top of the Empire State Building. Meanwhile, when he wasn't doing radio, he picked up work as a production assistant on movies and televsision commercials, hauling cables, driving vans, learning the craft of filmmaking.

On December 8, 1980, he was helping out with a commercial for the Hilton hotel on Sixth Avenue.

"As cold and shitty as it was," he'd recall, "when you're just out of school, working on a TV commercial in New York and getting paid, it really isn't that bad."

■   ■   ■

John and Yoko relaxed in the limo. It had been a good day—from the shoot with Annie Leibovitz to the radio interview to the productive time at the Record Plant—and now they were going home to end the night with their son. As the light from passing street lamps bounced on and off Yoko's skin, John glanced at his wife, thankful that everything had turned out this way.

Despite their devoted song lyrics, John and Yoko had not enjoyed a perfect marriage. Yoko's immense sadness over the disappearance of Kyoko, coupled with John's immigration problems and the backlash against some of the couple's political pronouncements engendered a chronic malaise. The two had been at a party on the night Richard Nixon was re-elected, and a bitter John—reeling from a combination of pills and alcohol—pulled a female guest into a room. Someone cranked up a Bob Dylan record to stifle the lovemaking grunts and spare Yoko any further humiliation.

At home, John seemed sexually unsatisfied. Aware that he'd been dependent on some sort of minder since the early days of Beatlemania, Yoko decided to set her husband free. If he wanted to rebel like an adolescent, the woman John called "Mother" decided, then he'd have to struggle like one.

John was dispatched to Los Angeles with an attractive, twenty-two-year-old assistant named May Pang. According to May, Yoko explicitly encouraged her to start dating John. May was a good person, Yoko reasoned, who would have a positive influence on John during the separation.

John's "Lost Weekend" would last fourteen months. He'd describe much of that period as a self-destructive odyssey with supporting characters like Ringo, Who drummer Keith Moon, and singer Harry Nilsson. At one point, this unholy triumvirate actually moved into a Santa Monica beach house with John and May Pang. "I'd be waking up drunk in strange places, or reading about myself in the paper, doing extraordinary things," John told *Rolling Stone*, "half of which I'd done, and half of which I hadn't done."

In some ways, John was again following the path blazed by his father, who'd often bragged of his six-month incarceration for busting open a shop window and drunkenly dancing with a mannequin in a wedding dress. One night, while dining out with Pang and Nilsson, John went into the ladies' room, emerging with a Kotex sanitary napkin affixed with perspiration to his forehead. The item remained there as the group headed to the Troubadour nightclub on Santa Monica Boulevard to see the Smothers Brothers' comedy act. There, John was so loud and obnoxious that the waitress refused to serve him.

"Do you know who I am?" he challenged.

"Yeah, you're some asshole with a Kotex on his head."

By his own admission, John had always clung to a degree of "immaturity," as a counter to conformity. But now, he told *Rolling Stone*, "there I am, doing the dumbest things... the things that I despise the most, almost, all to what? Avoid being normal?"

John and Yoko spoke daily. On the one hand, he was enjoying his tear. On the other, he wanted to come home. She told him he wasn't ready.

In the studio, John swigged vodka and fed off the agitated atmosphere created by Phil Spector. One session ended with an intoxicated John being dragged into a car, shouting his wife's name.

Spector's official task was producing *Rock 'n' Roll*—an album of some of John's favorite old tunes. But the "Wall of Sound" creator's unstable behavior didn't always inspire. The mood became so charged at one point that Spector pulled his ever-present pistol from his shoulder holster and put a bullet in the ceiling. Spector would become infamous for studio gunplay, pulling out his weapon and threatening the Ramones when he was working on their record *End of the Century* in 1980. Less than twenty years later he would be convicted of fatally shooting actress Lana Clarkson at his Los Angeles home.

Lennon appeared unafraid of the gunfire. But he reportedly reminded Spector, "Don't mess with my ears. I need them."

■ ■ ■

In the midst of his lost L.A. weekend and his fling with May Pang, John reconciled with estranged associates, including Paul McCartney. John was producing Harry Nilsson's *Pussy Cats* album when Paul and Linda walked into the Los Angeles Record Plant building. There was a momentary feeling of uncertainty until John proclaimed, "Valiant Paul McCartney, I presume."

He was alluding to a line from a Christmas play televised in the early days of Beatlemania.

"Sir Jaspar Lennon, I presume," replied Paul, immediately recognizing the reference.

The two politely shook hands and, for the only time since the Beatles' breakup, allowed themselves to be recorded together. Stevie Wonder was also in the studio, and he, John, and Harry Nilsson shared vocal chores while Paul sang harmony and played drums. Linda backed them up on the organ, and May Pang hit the tambourine. Wonder played electric piano, and Bobby Keyes, best known for performing with the Rolling Stones, played the saxophone.

The undertaking fell short of the bounty one expected from musicians of this dimension. John appeared to have difficulty with both his microphone and headphones, and seemed as preoccupied with cocaine as he was with the music.

"Do you want a snort, Stevie?" he could be heard on tape, asking Wonder. "A toot? It's going around."

Hence the name of the rarely noticed bootleg, *A Toot and a Snore in '74*.

Yet a barrier had been broken. When John was subsequently asked about Paul, his opinions tended to be more moderate. He'd refer to *Band on the Run* as a "great album." "Yesterday" was "beautiful." John understood that the former Beatles had their differences, but he was now willing to pick up a guitar and jam with any of them—no matter what had been said in the past. "We're all human," he told Pete Hamill in a 1975 *Rolling Stone* interview. "We can all change our minds."

The Beatles, in fact, "didn't break up because we weren't friends," he explained to Tom Snyder. "We just broke up over sheer boredom. And boredom creates tension."

■   ■   ■

On Pang's advice, John arranged for Julian to visit him—for the first time in four years—and purchased the boy a new guitar and drum set. Around Julian, John appeared sober and engaged. John and May had left L.A. and were living in New York with two cats. The young man remembered this period as one of the best between father and son.

In fact, eleven-year-old Julian played drums on the song "Ya Ya" on the 1974 *Walls and Bridges* album. May acted as the album's production coordinator while John generated hits like the enchanted "#9 Dream" and the droll "Whatever Gets You Through the Night"—featuring Elton John on harmony and keyboards.

By now, May Pang had fallen in love with John Lennon. Certainly, John felt a great deal of affection and gratitude toward May. But he still hoped to reconcile with Yoko. Because Yoko had given John the liberty to pursue other relationships, he encouraged her to date as well. As they discussed this topic on the phone, John noticed that his old feelings of jealousy and possessiveness had fallen away.

The theme of *Walls and Bridges* had been tearing down emotional barriers. Little by little, it appeared, the Lost Weekend had somehow helped John realize that goal.

After Elton John's collaboration with John—the two also worked on Elton's remake of "Lucy in the Sky with Diamonds," with Lennon singing in the chorus—the pair made a deal. If "Whatever Gets You Through the Night" ever hit #1, Lennon would join Elton on stage at one of his concerts. The former Beatle considered the possibility a long shot; he'd never had a #1 hit as a solo artist. But on November 16, 1974, the song reached the top of the *Billboard* charts.

Twelve days later, Elton John was in New York for a Thanksgiving concert at Madison Square Garden. As they had agreed, Lennon arrived backstage, prepared for his guest appearance.

John claimed to have no idea that Yoko would be there as well.

"I'd like to thank Elton and the boys for having me on tonight," John announced, after performing the two songs he'd recorded with Elton. "And we thought we'd do a number from an old estranged fiancé of mine called Paul. This is one I never sang."

Even before the two harmonized the first verse of "I Saw Her Standing There," the crowd in John's adopted hometown was frenzied. Later, some would wonder if, on this particular night, the title of the song related to Yoko.

"She was backstage afterwards," John told *Rolling Stone*, "and there was just that moment when we saw each other and . . . it's like in the movies, you know, when time stands still. And there was silence. Everything went silent . . . and we were just sort of looking at each other."

The reconciliation did not occur that night. But everyone who saw the couple knew that it was coming. May Pang claimed that she and John were planning a January trip to New Orleans, where Paul McCartney and Wings were recording *Venus and Mars*. But the day before the journey, Yoko apparently told John that she'd figured out a cure for his smoking habit.

John went home. "The separation didn't work out," he stated. "It's all right wondering what life is like on the other side and that's one of the lessons of life," he told New York's Capital Radio. "If you turn your head towards it, it goes away. I, like many other people, consciously look, whip my head round and find out I've banged my head into a wall."

He boasted that he, since reconnecting with Yoko, he felt "a bit sane again."

To *Rolling Stone*, he declared, "Alive in '75 is my new motto.... I've decided to want to live.... It's taken, however, many years, and I want to have a go at it."

13

HIBERNATION

On June 13, 1975, television viewers on both sides of the Atlantic watched a gum-chewing John—in a red jumpsuit and round, tinted glasses—perform "Slippin' and Slidin'" and "Imagine" during a special tribute to Sir Lew Grade, the British media mogul who owned most of the Beatles' song catalog.

Instead of intoning "no religion," Lennon sang, "no immigration, too."

He would never appear on stage again.

Yoko was pregnant, he told friends, and he needed to concentrate on taking this second round of fatherhood seriously. At forty-three, Yoko had been told that she was too old to conceive, and that in any case John's past drug abuse would neutralize his sperm. Determined to start a family, Yoko found a Chinese acupuncturist in San Francisco who assured her that if she ate well, and shunned alcohol and drugs, she would give birth within eighteen months.

Shortly before the acupuncturist died, the Lennons sent him a Polaroid of their newborn child.

"We worked hard for that child," John told *Playboy*. "We went though all hell trying to have a baby, through many miscarriages and other problems. He is what they call a love child, in truth."

Adding to the wonder of the event was the fact that the boy was born on John's thirty-fifth birthday. The couple chose the name Sean—the Irish version of John—in tribute to the Lennon family's Celtic origins.

In another symbolic gesture, Elton John—the man John held responsible for generating his reconciliation with Yoko—was named as the baby's godfather.

"I feel higher than the Empire State Building," John told the press that morning, referencing one of the most conspicuous landmarks in the city John now regarded as his own.

As Sean was approaching his first birthday, the family flew to Japan to visit Yoko's relatives. At a press conference at the Hotel Okura, the couple officially announced their sabbatical from show business.

Said John, "We've basically decided, without a great decision, to be with our baby as much as we can, until we feel we can take the time off to indulge ourselves, creating things outside the family."

Since age twenty-two, John had been locked into some type of recording contract. "After all those years, it was all I knew," he told *Playboy*. "I wasn't free. I was boxed in. My contract was the physical manifestation of being in prison.... Rock 'n' roll wasn't fun anymore."

John no longer listened to his songs, claiming that each reminded him of the particular recording sessions, as well as the studio and industry infighting. For a period, John wondered if he'd ever record music again, imagining a second career as a children's book author. "I've always had the feeling of giving what *Wind in the Willows* and *Alice in Wonderland* and *Treasure Island* gave to me at age seven or eight," he told Pete Hamill, "the books that really opened my whole being."

For the short term, John looked after Sean—wrestling together, playing with the cats, taking carriage rides in Central Park—and baked bread, feeling the same satisfaction at watching the loaves rise, he joked, as he would at receiving a gold record.

At night, Sean would watch *The Muppet Show*, then go into his room to play with his plastic airplanes. Then John would enter, turning the light off and on with each syllable while enunciating, "Good. Night. Sean."

Later on, Sean would be able to distinguish between the fabled figure named John Lennon and the loving man who stood in his bedroom. "My dad is who I remember playing with as a child," he told *People*. "I remember his voice, his touch, his smell."

When John ran into a celebrity friend in Manhattan, he'd point at Sean and say, "I would like you to meet my guru." "He always called Sean his guru," recounted Peter Boyle, the *Young Frankenstein* actor who'd hung out with John during his Lost Weekend phase. "He just loved walking around New York. . . . He did not want to live as most rock stars and movie stars do, behind a wall of bodyguards."

Yoko noted that most New Yorkers instinctively understood John's decision to live among them, and gave the family the space they needed to feel relaxed. "New Yorkers are really tops," she told the *New York Press*. "I think that all of us feel that we are sharing this town and, in that sense, we are sort of family, and we care for each other."

As before their breakup, John and Yoko seemed fastened to each other. "John once said, 'They say that the gods are jealous of lovers and would try to split them,'" Yoko revealed in *People*. "But they wouldn't do that to us. We wouldn't let them.' When we were walking outside, we always held hands, as if we were afraid of being separated."

To Mick Jagger, it seemed as if his old friend "went into hibernation." Jagger had occasionally joined Lennon and his posse on their Lost Weekend outings, and knew a number of people at the Dakota. Even though John had told everyone that he was cutting ties to the music business, Jagger believed their camaraderie transcended the trade. When Mick stopped in at the Dakota, he'd leave Lennon a note, asking if he wanted to chat for a little while. John never replied.

Lennon would take McCartney's phone calls, although Paul was never sure if the acidic John would suddenly materialize. Still, like the brothers they'd become, their history was deep enough to get past it. If John didn't feel like talking about music, Paul was content listening to his former band mate's stories about Sean, supplementing them with tales of the McCartney kids.

From time to time, Paul would turn up at John's apartment with a guitar in his hand. The two would play music, joke about mutual acquaintances and watch television. On April 24, 1976, the two were watching *Saturday Night Live* on NBC when creator Lorne Michaels looked into the lens and suddenly addressed the four former Beatles, asking them to reunite on his show:

> We've heard and read a lot about personality and legal con-
> flicts.... That's something that's none of my business....
> You guys will have to handle that. But it's also been said
> that no one has yet to come up with enough money to satisfy
> you. Well, if it's money you want, there's no problem here.

He then held up a check for $3,000—authorized, he said, by the benevolence of the National Broadcasting Corporation. "All you have to do is sing three Beatles songs," Michaels continued. "'She loves you, yeah, yeah, yeah.' That's $1,000 right there. You know the words. It'll be easy. Like I said, this is made out to the Beatles. You divide it up any way you want. If you want to give less to Ringo, that's up to you."

Paul and John were completely amused, and actually contemplated hailing a taxi and bursting onto the set. But John claimed that the old partners were too tired to shock the world that night.

■　■　■

For the first four years of Sean's life, John would walk by the unusual guitar he'd hung up in his bedroom—a contraption that expanded and contracted depending on whether the player was standing up or sitting down—and more or less ignore it. Tickled with its novelty, he'd purchased the instrument around the time that he and Yoko had reunited. Now he was too submerged in childcare to give it much thought.

As Sean's attention began to shift toward school and friends, the guitar became more conspicuous. John thought about the way it would sound on an album, and how much fun it would be to play on stage. In an interview with *Newsweek*, he playfully described his sentiments: "This housewife would like to have a career for a bit."

John discussed these feelings with Yoko, and she understood. She was an artist herself, and knew that creative impulses could only be contained for a finite amount of time. She'd also been thinking of music—songs she wanted to write, songs she wanted to record.

Together, the Lennons decided to become entertainers again.

"We feel like doing it," John explained to *Playboy*, "and we have something to say."

In the spring of 1980—while Yoko stayed home dealing with the couple's investments, philanthropic endeavors, and other concerns—John sailed a sloop to Bermuda with a small crew, listening to contemporary performers like Madness, the Pretenders, and Lene Lovich while at sea. Shortly after John arrived, Sean and his nanny flew down to join him. During the day, father and son swam, went sightseeing, and played on the beach; when John was alone, he was as relaxed as he'd ever been in his life. One night, he went to a dance club, more to observe than anything else, and spotted a group of vacationers laughing and dancing to the B-52s' warbling tune "Rock Lobster."

He shook his head and smiled to himself. "This sounds like Yoko's music," he said aloud.

Indeed, the B-52s *were* Yoko Ono fans, just like Elvis Costello and the future members of Sonic Youth. Everything had suddenly aligned. Instead of being perceived as a kook, Yoko was receiving her due as an innovator.

It took a while, but the world was catching up.

At a botanical garden, John and Sean saw an orchid called a double fantasy. John loved the name. To him, it was an ideal to which every couple should aspire—each partner contented because the other was meeting needs that had previously been romanticized.

John called Yoko. They had to do another album. For the next three weeks, John would write a song and sing it over the phone to Yoko. She'd then respond by writing her own tune, as part of a long-distance musical dialogue. John also tinkered with tunes he'd begun conceptualizing at the Dakota. By the time he returned home, the pair had come up with twenty-five songs— enough for *Double Fantasy* and more.

Yoko approached producer Jack Douglas, the engineer from *Imagine* who'd since worked with Patti Smith, Cheap Trick, the New York Dolls, and Aerosmith, among others. Jack listened to the demos recorded at the Dakota. He realized that he'd have to be careful to avoid overproducing this album; he didn't want to reduce any of the authenticity.

In August 1980, the production of the LP began in earnest. "(Just Like) Starting Over" was John and Yoko's attempt to trace their relationship through its various stages, both exhilarating and painful. The song was an emotional one for the artists; as they reflected on their early infatuation and idealism, they realized just how many sixties couples they knew had broken up, splintering their families in the process.

It didn't have to be that way, the song stressed.

At the very beginning of the song, a bell could be heard quietly ringing. It was the sound of Yoko's wishing bell, not unlike the type used in Buddhist ceremonies to tempt feelings of hope. "It's like at the beginning of 'Mother,'" John told *Rolling Stone*, "which had a very slow death bell. So it's taken a long time to get from a slow, church death bell to this sweet little wishing bell.... To me, my work is one piece."

■　■　■

When "(Just Like) Starting Over" became the album's first single, the couple chose Yoko's "Kiss, Kiss, Kiss" for the B-side. Mixed into the New Wave rhythm was the sound of what appeared to be a woman having an orgasm, then crying out to be held. This was Yoko's addendum to the philosophy espoused on the A-side. Beyond the sex, Yoko emphasized, every woman carried a hunger for that genuine touch.

"Watching the Wheels" was John's explanation for devoting himself to his family. There was nothing vague about the song. The lyrics read as if the former Beatle were discussing his choices with a friend. Although many questioned the logic of withdrawing from the industry, he essentially said, he needed to focus on those fundamental truths too often obscured by celebrity.

The news about *Double Fantasy* had trickled out slowly, starting as a rumor that John and Yoko were working on something again. As the stories gained velocity, record companies began bidding for Lennon's comeback album. John and Yoko were in the power position now, and wouldn't have to compromise creatively or financially. Because they regarded David Geffen as a man rooted in the future, rather than in the muddled traditions of the industry, they endowed their trust in his new label.

Like the music, the album's cover art needed to reflect the couple's personal journey. Japanese erotic photographer Kishin Shinoyama photographed the pair in a black-and-white style reminiscent of Astrid Kirchherr's pictures from Hamburg. In his home country, Shinoyama was alternately revered and disdained.

John was happy to work with someone who understood him.

■   ■   ■

Chapman wondered if his bullets would work. They'd been back and forth through the airport x-ray machine so many times, buried at the bottom of the suitcase. Maybe they'd been damaged somehow. Mark would pull out the pistol and, then—nothing.

But maybe not. Chapman tingled with excitement, imaging his infamy. He glanced over at photographer Paul Goresh. The guy had no idea.

Over the past few days, Chapman had developed an affinity toward Goresh. They'd both started off as Beatles fans who took their passion further than most others. The difference was that Goresh had managed to become John Lennon's friend. Chapman wondered why something like that hadn't happened to him.

Darkness had fallen, and Goresh prepared to leave the Dakota and head home to New Jersey. Chapman asked him to reconsider.

"You never know," Chapman said. "Something might happen to him, and you'll never see him again."

Goresh seemed confused by the comment. "What do you mean?" he replied. "I see John Lennon all the time."

Chapman hesitated. He had the gun in his pocket. Now wasn't the time to give away too much. One stupid remark and he could be in handcuffs before he even made his statement.

"Well, you never know," Chapman stammered. "He may go to Spain and you'll never see him again."

Goresh shrugged, indicating that the possibility didn't trouble him. He said goodbye to Chapman and headed home.

Later, some would wonder whether Chapman had wanted the photographer to chronicle the deed. But that wasn't what Chapman was thinking—Goresh represented a friendly presence who might somehow reroute Chapman from his mission. But now he was gone.

The little people were quiet.

The options were running out.

■   ■   ■

It had taken his entire life, but John could finally walk in the same shoes as his Aunt Mimi.

As a father, he now understood the immense responsibility she felt as the woman essentially in charge of John's upbringing. And he was thankful. Years earlier, he'd purchased his aunt a coastal home in the southern English town of Dorset. But he knew that she was getting older, and wanted to bring Sean over to see her. Maybe he'd even visit with Julian on the same trip.

Over the weekend, John had phoned his aunt, telling her of his plans.

"You come over any time," she told him.

They laughed about the past and her aversion to his career goals. "I never thought there was a future in strumming the guitar," she said. "But you must have been right in the end."

■   ■   ■

Over the past few years, Paul had become the most successful musician in modern history—some 3,500 artists would cover "Yesterday" alone. In 1977, Paul's "Mull of Kintyre," a bagpipe-laden accolade to his Hibernian heritage, became the first single to sell more than two million copies in Great Britain—and the country's best-selling non-charity single ever. Yet, John was no longer begrudging. Paul called John before the release of *Double Fantasy* to offer congratulations. John knew when Paul was jiving, and this time, he wasn't.

The words were sincere.

There was so much admiration between these former enemies that they began to consider a scene that John had repeatedly vowed would never occur—a Beatles concert, possibly across the street from his home, in Central Park.

■   ■   ■

Alan Weiss, the senior program producer for WABC News, removed his full-face motorcycle helmet as he stood in front of the ATM, withdrawing the money he'd need for his date that night. He stuffed the cash in his pocket and headed back to his motorcy-cle—the one his station had purchased to courier footage from the site of a story during the New York City transit strike. Placing the helmet back on, Alan neglected to strap it under his chin.

Although rush hour was technically over, there was still a good deal of traffic in midtown, given the Rockefeller Center Christmas tree lighting and other factors, but Alan knew how to circumvent it. He revved up the motorcycle and wound south toward Park Drive, the road bisecting Central Park. "They say there are two types of motorcycle drivers," he said, "those who've had accidents, and those who are about to. But I was always pretty careful."

On Park Drive, he hugged the perimeter of the road, heading toward Central Park South and Seventh Avenue. Suddenly, the taxi driver in the middle lane had second thoughts about leaving the park, cutting to the left while Alan was cutting right. "You don't need Newton to know that two bodies of matter can't occupy the same space at the same time," Alan would recollect. His front tire slammed into the taxi, sending him hurtling over the handlebars, bumping against the hood and windshield.

"I hit the ground like a rock skimming across a lake," he said. "Because I hadn't buckled on my helmet, it slipped off, and my head banged the ground a few times."

When he came to a stop, he contemplated his condition:

> I said, "I'm alive. I'm in one piece. I think I'm okay." I look west and, as if on cue, all four lanes of traffic seemed like they had cars in them. I'm laying on the road, and my outfit is complete and total black. I don't have anything on me that's reflective. I go to get up, and I can't move my right leg. It's amazing—you read about adrenaline. I just got up on one leg and threw myself off the roadway, away from the cars, onto the grass.

The taxi driver was decent enough to pull over and radio for an ambulance. In the meantime, citizens appeared out of nowhere, offering reassuring words. "You hear all these stories about New Yorkers not being friendly," Alan said. "This is going on at ten o'clock at night in a poorly lit area of Central Park. Nobody mugged me. Everybody helped me."

When the EMTs arrived, they concluded that Alan had a fractured hip. As they loaded him onto the ambulance, one of the attendants looked down at Alan and nodded: "Man, are you lucky. It's Monday night, and it's slow in the ER. If this was the weekend, with all the shootings, you'd be in that hospital for hours before anyone saw you."

■   ■   ■

The crowd at Madison Square Garden rose to its feet, stomping, cheering, and screaming. World Wide Wrestling Federation tag-team champions Rick Martel and his partner Tony Garea came to the ring with their title belts strapped around their waists, slapping hands all the way from the dressing room. When they stepped through the ropes, they turned toward the photographers crouched at ringside—mainly American guys, but a few Japanese working for the weekly, glossy-covered wrestling magazines published in Tokyo—and posed for pictures.

This was going to be easy.

Their opponents, Afa and Sika, "The Wild Samoans," paced the opposite side of the ring, shaking the ropes and twisting their faces as their manager, "Captain" Lou Albano, muttered in their ears.

Martel—a tanned French Canadian with a high-voltage smile— loved working with the Samoans because they could instantly rile up the crowd. For big men, they moved quickly. They chopped hard—the sound of flesh reverberating around the building, creating a sense of believability. And, when facing a guy of Martel's caliber, they weren't hesitant about "selling," rolling across the ring and acting hurt when he caught them with a dropkick or flying head scissors.

"I wrestled the Samoans everywhere," Martel remembered, "Washington, D.C.; Philly; Portland, Maine. People liked watching our matches because they could tell the Samoans were pretty tough guys. In fact, I'd seen Sika in Montreal, walking around barefoot in the snow.

"In wrestling, everybody lives their gimmick to a degree. But Afa and Sika were the real thing. They were a class apart."

The bell rang, and Rick locked up with Afa. Grunting, with his feral hair waving, the Samoan twisted his opponent's nose and gouged at his eyes. The crowd loudly booed, and both men were satisfied.

This was Madison Square Garden. With the tree lighting over, nothing bigger was happening in New York City on a cold winter night.

■ ■ ■

The commuter train rolled on elevated tracks through the Bronx, then crossed out of the city into Westchester County. Normally, Adam Shanker, the Knickerbocker Pub bartender, would feel self-conscious, reading *Playboy* magazine on the train, in public. But the John and Yoko interview just fascinated him.

When asked by reporter David Sheff to define his dream for the eighties, John urged readers to "make your own dream.... Don't expect Jimmy Carter or Ronald Reagan or Yoko Ono or Bob Dylan or Jesus Christ to come and do it for you. You have to do it yourself.... I can't wake you up. You can wake you up. I can't cure you. You can cure you."

Only later would a tiny incident that occurred during the interview be analyzed for its perverse irony. As John and Yoko considered a question from Sheff, they were interrupted by the sound of a car backfiring outside their apartment.

Quipped Lennon, "Another murder at Rue Dakota."

14

No Way to Fix It

Mark David Chapman was sitting inside the Dakota archway. His heart fluttered. As he gazed catty-corner across West Seventy-second Street toward Central Park, he spotted a limousine slowing to a halt at the stop light. It was 10:50 P.M., and Chapman sensed that the moment had arrived.

"I had a clear mind as to what I was going to do," he'd recall. "I believe I was under compulsion, but my mind was very clear."

The wind was blowing hard against Chapman's face, but the frigidity didn't register. A peculiar feeling of calm overtook him. "Do it," a voice urged from inside. "Do it. Do it."

The limo pulled up in front of the building. Had it continued into the Dakota's courtyard, Chapman would have missed his former idol. But John and Yoko had gotten into the habit of exiting at the curb and greeting fans on the way inside.

The building's doorman, Jose Perdomo, was on the sidewalk, all but oblivious to Chapman. A cab driver sat in his vehicle in front of the building after dropping off a passenger. The Dakota's elevator operator stared past Chapman, toward the street. Yoko walked ahead of her husband, pleased with their efforts at the Record Plant and looking forward to seeing her son. A relaxed John trailed some thirty feet behind her, holding the session tapes. When he spotted Chapman, John made eye contact, recognizing the visitor from their exchange earlier in the day.

Waiting for John to pass by, Chapman started toward the street, as if he were done for the night. He counted his steps—*one, two, three, four, five.*

Then he wheeled around and pulled out the .38.

Chapman went into a combat stance—just like at the shooting range—aimed at John's back, and squeezed the trigger.

One of the hollow-points passed over John's head, shattering a window at the Dakota.

Chapman kept going. Two more bullets pierced the singer's back, on the left side. Another two penetrated his left shoulder.

At least one of the projectiles cut into Lennon's aorta.

"That's it," Chapman said to himself, letting the gun hang limply at his side. He couldn't believe that he'd actually followed through on his plan.

Yoko ran for cover. John staggered up the six steps into the building's security area. "I'm shot," he muttered, and crumpled onto the ground, blood dribbling from his mouth.

Chapman stood there, watching Yoko rush over to her husband and cradle his body.

Concierge Jay Hastings took off his uniform jacket, placing it on the former Beatle's bloodied chest, and removed John's glasses.

Neither Hastings nor Yoko looked at Chapman. All their focus was on John. Now that the firing had stopped, they didn't even seem afraid of the gunman.

He really *was* a nobody.

Chapman heard what he'd describe as a "blood-curdling scream." This wasn't Yoko making art. This was her crying for the love of her life.

Chapman would later tell Larry King that the noise "put the hair on the back of my neck straight up."

"John's been shot!" she yelled. "John's been shot!"

Tears filled Jose Perdomo's eyes, as he stomped up to Chapman. "I felt so sorry for Jose," the shooter would recollect. The doorman grabbed Chapman's right wrist and shook his arm. The gun fell from Chapman's grip onto the ground.

Chapman thought ahead. He knew that the police would be coming, and he didn't want them to frisk him too roughly. He removed his coat, so it wouldn't appear that he had weapons hidden in the bulky material. He also took off his hat. He placed both on the sidewalk, but held onto his copy of *The Catcher in the Rye*.

Perdomo was incredulous. "Do you know what you've done?!" he shouted.

"Yes, I just shot John Lennon."

He looked down at the book, and tried to read. He was nervous, could still smell the gunpowder, and began to pace. He wanted the police to get there.

He later claimed to feel "devastated" over what he'd done: "I believe that if I really wanted to, I could have changed my mind. I had ample opportunity to do it and I didn't do it, and I regret that deeply."

■　■　■

At the Langham Building on Central Park West, just a block north of the Dakota, singer James Taylor was on the phone with a friend in Los Angeles. When James was just twenty years old, the Beatles had embraced Taylor and released his debut album on their Apple label. He had always felt a connection to John. Recently Taylor and his wife, Carly Simon, had bumped into John and Yoko at a dance performance and they had all had their picture taken together. Yoko, especially, could not have been friendlier.

Taylor's conversation was interrupted by what he thought were a series of gunshots. Given his old-school counterculture sensibility, he assumed that it was the police who were wielding the weapons.

■　■　■

From Ellen Chesler's second-story apartment, on the Seventy-third Street side of the Dakota, the sound of gunfire echoed so loudly that she knew it was close.

She had been warming a bottle of milk for her six-month-old daughter. Now she grabbed the baby and ran out of the room.

Her husband called the concierge for details. Remarkably, Jay Hastings picked up and said that John Lennon had been shot.

"Please," Hastings said, "call the police."

■ ■ ■

Officers Peter Cullen and Steve Spiro were at Seventy-second and Broadway when they received a call about possible shots fired at the Dakota. Spiro was in the driver's seat, and stepped on the gas.

"Take it a little easy," Cullen cautioned. "It could be fireworks in Central Park or something."

The car flew. The cops arrived at the Dakota within seconds. As Spiro shifted into park, Cullen noticed someone running from the building. But this wasn't a perp. This was an honest citizen, frightened by what he'd just witnessed.

"Officer, be careful," the man yelled, as Cullen exited the vehicle. "There's a guy in the alleyway there, shooting a gun."

Cullen and Spiro were not steady partners, and usually took opposite sides on union issues. But each had the other's back, and neither had to verbalize what needed to be done next. Each man approached the driveway from the opposite side. "Everyone's frozen, standing there," Cullen recalled. "We don't see anyone on the floor. We don't see signs of anything. I see a fella with a shirt and tie on, and I see Jose the doorman—the only guy I knew."

"Jose, what's going on?" Cullen asked.

Perdomo pointed. "He shot John Lennon."

The officer's eyes followed the line of the doorman's finger. The conservative guy appeared to be embroiled in some type of disagreement with a Hispanic man in dirty clothes. The Hispanic guy was agitated, gesturing, speaking in some hybrid of Spanish and English.

Cullen pointed his gun at the man.

"*No*," Jose corrected. "Not him. That's our handyman." He gestured at Chapman. "*Him!*"

Spiro put the suspect against the wall, and began frisking him. "Where's Lennon?" Cullen asked Jose.

"The bullets pushed him through the door." He motioned at the security station. "Over there." Once again, the doorman began to tear up. "That's the father of a five-year-old kid."

Chapman offered no resistance to Spiro. So Cullen said, "Steve, hold on to this guy." He walked toward the security area, noticing a highly agitated Asian woman. The officer immediately realized that this was Yoko Ono, but he couldn't think about that. In the security entrance, the ex-Beatle was facedown on the rug, bleeding from the mouth.

"Steve," Cullen hollered to his partner. "Put the cuffs on him."

Chapman put both hands on his head, blocking his face with his forearms.

"Don't hurt me," he begged.

"No one's going to hurt you." Spiro placed Chapman's hands against the wall, frisked and handcuffed the suspect.

Mark looked at his copy of *The Catcher in the Rye* on the ground. "Could you please pick up my book?" he asked quietly.

■   ■   ■

The officers called for backup, and several more patrol cars arrived. Lennon looked terrible—so bloody, he was barely recognizable—but he was still alive, and needed to get to the hospital quickly. No one wanted to wait for an ambulance. So Police Officer Tony Palma grabbed John's arms, and his partner, Herb Frauenberger, hoisted up the victim's legs, hauling him to a patrol car and laying him across the back seat.

Today, this breach of protocol—lifting a body before medics and the fire department arrived—would yield fines and suspensions. But none of the officers were concerned about procedure. "You had a life to save here," Cullen explained.

Yoko snapped out of her misery to question the strategy. "Do you think you should move him?" she asked.

"Lady," Frauenberger responded, "if we don't move him now, he'll die for sure."

Recalled Cullen, "Without an ambulance there, what are you going to do—stand over him and start praying?"

Once Lennon was situated in the vehicle, the cops looked around, and realized that other patrol cars were boxing them in. So they moved Lennon a second time, and placed him in another cruiser.

Officer Jim Moran was at the wheel—his partner rode shotgun. No one was in the back seat with John Lennon. They took off toward Roosevelt Hospital.

Moran noticed that, already, people on the street knew what had occurred, shouting the Beatle's name at the patrol car. Moran glanced at the bloodied figure in the back seat, trying to keep him engaged—and alive.

"Do you know who you are?" the officer asked.

John emitted a gurgling groan, and nodded.

Moran radioed Roosevelt: "Have paramedics meet us at the emergency entrance."

Tony Palma and Herb Frauenberger took Yoko to their hospital. They peered at her through the rearview mirror, observing a scared, helpless woman. Yoko said nothing to the cops, and they said nothing to her. They'd been through this routine before, and words couldn't change the outcome.

Outside the Dakota, Spiro was still standing with Chapman. "I acted alone," the suspect offered, repudiating whatever conspiracy theories might arise later on.

■　■　■

"Don't let anyone hurt me," Chapman begged. "Stay with me."

Neither of the officers felt merciful enough to reassure the suspect.

"I'm sorry," Chapman continued. "I didn't mean to give you a hard time, and ruin your night."

Cullen and Spiro looked at one another with disbelief. "You're apologizing to us?" Cullen spouted. "You know what you just did? You screwed up your whole life. What the hell's the matter with you?"

"I didn't have anything against him. I don't know why I did it."

"Then, what did you do it for?"

"The Big Man inside of me is Holden Caulfield. The small part is the Devil. And tonight, the small part won."

■　■　■

Chapman told the cops that the Big Man had scored previous victories, when Chapman lacked the courage to shoot his prey. Oddly, Cullen could follow the suspect's logic. Clearly, Chapman had some delusions, but, in the officer's estimate, he was "not too crazy. And he was polite. He wasn't all, 'hey, muthafucka,' and all that shit. Dressed very nicely. If he was walking down the street with three other guys, he might've been the last one I'd expect to shoot me."

At the precinct, Spiro courteously offered the collar to Cullen: "You should take this."

"No, Steve. It should be you."

Despite their differences, both were trying to be deferential. Cullen was anticipating a promotion to sergeant, and believed that Spiro needed the collar more.

"Take this arrest," he implored. "Don't worry about it. It's good for you—you'll have this on your record the rest of your life. I'm going to be sergeant soon. I don't need this."

Ultimately, the men agreed to share the credit.

By then, Ted Turner's fledgling Cable News Network (CNN) had reported that John Lennon had been shot—condition unknown.

■　■　■

Ken Dashow—"Cousin Ken"—slammed the white paneled van door shut. The Hilton commercial shoot had gone well. Now it was his job, as the production assistant, to drive from one twenty-four-hour equipment house to another, dropping off the camera, the tripod, the dolly, the sandbags.

He steered uptown, toward someplace on Amsterdam Avenue, listening to New York's classic rock station, WNEW. At about Seventieth Street, he stopped at a light and noticed a trickle of people running up Central Park West. Then came more, and more and more.

"Traffic's not moving," he described the scene later. "They're running and crying. I hear sirens somewhere. I'm nervous, thinking, 'This has got to be a bomb scare. It's looking dangerous.'"

Nothing moved for fifteen minutes or so. Then a police officer arrived and directed the cars downtown. "It didn't dawn on me to even turn on news radio," Ken said. "It's just not something I ever listened to."

■   ■   ■

Regulars at the Lion's Head in Greenwich Village were occasionally told that the bar was a refuge for writers with drinking problems. The common retort was that the saloon was really a sanctuary for drinkers with writing problems.

It was a cozy place decorated with a hundred or so or so framed covers of books authored by regulars. The Posties—or *New York Post* guys—hung out there after work, as opposed to Costello's, where the *Daily News* reporters congregated. But now the merriment in the Lion's Head was interrupted by the news that something had happened to John Lennon.

Everyone tried to sober up and form some kind of working strategy. George Arzt, the City Hall bureau chief, had a brain-storm. Didn't Ellen Chesler—the city council president's chief of staff—live in the Dakota?

George had her home phone number. What a lucky break! He maneuvered over to the saloon's pay phone. One of the police reporters was on the phone. As soon as the guy hung up, George dialed Ellen.

She picked up. Yes, she'd heard the gunshots. And her husband had called 911. She even thought she'd seen the gunman, hanging out in front of the building, waiting for John Lennon, for days. George scribbled everything down, then phoned his desk.

"I felt the pressure of a deadline coming on," he said, "and the need to get the story in the paper. And I felt a certain excitement, getting my name on a John Lennon story."

■   ■   ■

"I don't know whether to diagnose you or plant you."

Alan Weiss looked down at his dirt-caked wounds and laughed at the emergency room doctor's joke. She asked her patient to repeat the tale of his motorcycle crash. When he finished, she told him, "We'll have to take you for x-rays before we can do anything. We have to see what the story is with your hip."

"Great," Alan answered. "When can we go?"

Before she could reply, the doors of the emergency room slammed open so violently that it felt as if the entire hospital was shaking.

"Gunshot!" a voice called out. "We've got a gunshot—gunshot to the chest!"

The doctor looked away. "I'm sorry, Alan," she said, starting toward the commotion, "I need to take care of this. It could be a while."

"That's okay, Doc. I'm not going anywhere."

From his gurney, Weiss positioned his body to watch the mayhem; even as a patient, he was still a news person. A group of police officers flanked a stretcher as they raced through the emergency room.

"This one!" a doctor yelled, pointing at the private room next to Alan.

Weiss closed his eyes, imagining the patient as a victim of a drug deal gone bad. He exhaled. This *was* going to take a long time.

Two of the cops came out of the room, chatting as if Alan were a lighting fixture. "Jesus," said one of the officers. "Can you believe it? John Lennon."

Alan opened his eyes, and bent his neck forward. "Excuse me, sir," he interrupted. "What did you say?"

"Nothing. I said nothing."

Alan observed the cops, as they repaired to a more private spot to continue their conversation. Did they say Jim Lennon? John Lemon? Or John Lennon, the Beatle?

Maybe it was Jack Lemmon, although that didn't seem to make much sense.

For a moment, anyway, Alan stopped thinking about his hip.

■　■　■

Jack Douglas never left the Record Plant. There was plenty to do there, and he liked working late. David Geffen had gone home earlier, ecstatic. It had been another good day.

Suddenly, Jack's girlfriend charged into the studio. She was out of breath. Before he could speak, she told him that she'd been listening to the radio.

His friend, John Lennon, had been shot.

■　■　■

Keith Richards was downtown when he first heard about the attack. He didn't worry too much—John and his friends in the Rolling Stones had tempted death so many times that Richards was certain Lennon would emerge with a few scars and a good story.

■　■　■

At the hospital, Dr. Richard Marks gave the John Lennon an open-heart massage. Lennon didn't have any blood pressure, and Marks ordered blood transfusions to bring it back.

Nothing appeared to be helping.

Just outside the door, Weiss wasn't sure if he'd been hallucinating. Maybe he'd banged his head too hard in the accident. But he felt that he should call the news desk and tell them his theory.

From the stretcher, Alan watched a man sweep the floor. Weiss motioned him forward, handing him a business card and twenty-dollar bill.

"Can you do me a favor? Could you call this number and ask for Neil?" Neil Goldstein was the assignment editor at WABC. "Tell him Alan Weiss is in the hospital, Roosevelt Hospital, and he thinks John Lennon may have been shot. Can you do that for me?"

"Sure."

Alan rested on the stretcher. He'd done his job. "I had probable cause," he later said. "I responded to it. I can't do anything else."

Five minutes passed. Alan's head throbbed. Suddenly, a booming voice commanded his attention.

"Mr. Weiss?"

A large man in a security jacket hovered over him. "Here's your twenty dollars," the guy said. "Here's your card. No personal calls."

Debating the whole issue of the public's right to know was out of the question. Alan felt sleazy: "Here someone's life is hanging by a thread next to me, and I'm adding unnecessary noise to the situation."

A woman's cry cut through the air. Weiss followed the sound. A mammoth cop was escorting an Asian woman in a full-length mink coat through the emergency room. There were lots of women who looked like Yoko Ono in New York. Alan wasn't sure if he could pick her out of a lineup. But the odds were starting to weigh in that direction.

Gazing at the other gurneys scattered across the room, he came up with a plan. He'd hop, one-legged, to the pay phone in the waiting area, using the stretchers as support. Then, he'd call Neil himself.

"I get all the way to the door," he remembered. "I'm turning the doorknob when, suddenly, I feel this vise grip on my upper arm. It was another big security guard. They only hired big security guards in hospitals."

Alan wasn't getting to the pay phone. "What are you doing?" the guard demanded.

"I'm going to make a phone call."

"You can't."

"Excuse me."

"You can't make a phone call."

Alan felt indignant. "You let go of me right now, or I'll have you arrested for assault."

It was an idle threat, and the guard knew it. Without speaking, he pulled the hopping patient back toward the gurney. Out of nowhere, Alan spotted one of the cops who'd brought him to the hospital. They made eye contact. The officer looked at the security guard.

"Let him go."

Now, the cop wanted an explanation. "Don't you know?" Weiss asked.

"Don't I know what?"

"That John Lennon's been shot."

"Who told you that?"

"No one exactly told me. I just heard two police officers talking."

The cop laughed. "Alan," he started. "You hit your head really hard. If John Lennon was shot, believe me, I would've heard about it."

By now, the pair was situated by the nursing stand. "Look, officer," Alan pleaded, "would you do me a favor? Could I just make one phone call?"

The cop picked up the phone and dialed WABC. After briefly describing his accident, Weiss told Neil Goldstein his theory. "I think I've seen Yoko Ono," the patient said.

The assignment editor listened. "You know," he replied. "I heard a call on the scanner for an ambulance up to Seventy-second and Central Park West. I knew the Dakota was over there, and sent a crew. There are a lot of famous people in that building...."

"That's it," Weiss cut in. "It's John Lennon. This is the last piece of the puzzle."

"You mean, he's really been shot?"

"Yes, he's really been shot."

Hanging up, Alan allowed the cop to help him to the gurney. He lay down, listening to the frenzied activity in the adjoining room. Sitting up, Weiss stretched his body and peeked through the open door.

"I'm looking into the room," he said. "John Lennon has no clothes on. His feet are facing me. His chest is open. It felt like I was looking into his chest, but there was blood all over, and all sorts of wires and tubes." Alan wondered if he was hallucinating.

Before he could speculate further, a group of security officers converged on the gurney. "Mr. Weiss," one said, "we have to move you."

"No. I'm fine right here."

"Lie down."

The guard's tone compelled Alan to comply. He was quickly wheeled out of the emergency room into the hallway, away from the dying Beatle.

■ ■ ■

Dr. Stephen Lynn knew the Lennons by sight. Their children went to the same school. From time to time, the doctor and his family would visit a Japanese restaurant at Sixty-ninth Street and Columbus Avenue, and see Sean there with his parents. Lynn never approached John directly. But he'd heard good things about him—things that had nothing to do with the Beatles. John and Yoko didn't always publicize their charitable contributions to the community, but the people on the Upper West Side knew.

Lynn had been called in to work to treat a man with multiple gunshot wounds, never fathoming the scene he'd encounter. Yoko sat on the ground as Lynn and two other doctors tried to save her husband. "The bullets were amazingly well-placed," he told the *New York Times*. "All the major blood vessels leaving the heart were a mush, and there was no way to fix it."

Lennon had neither a pulse nor blood pressure. He had gone into hypovolemic shock, the result of losing some eighty percent of his blood volume.

There was nothing more to be done.

At 11:15 P.M., John Lennon was officially pronounced dead.

■　■　■

The death certificate described the cause of death: "multiple gunshot wounds of left shoulder and chest; left lung and left subclavian artery; external and internal hemorrhage. Shock."

Chief Medical Examiner Elliot Gross would later say that no one could survive more than a few minutes in this kind of condition.

"Homicide" was listed as a contributory cause.

Yoko banged her head on the floor. "It can't be," she told Lynn. "He was just alive. Twenty minutes ago, we were in the car."

The doctor worried for the widow's safety. But she had to compose herself. She wasn't just a wife, she was a mother.

As Yoko was handed John's wedding ring, her thoughts turned to Sean, at home with his nanny. What if he was watching television and the broadcast was interrupted? The little boy needed his mother. Who else could tell him the unbelievable news that his father—one of the most loved figures on earth—had been shot to death underneath the boy's window?

By a fan.

Dr. Lynn assured Yoko that he'd wait until she arrived home to tell the world that John was dead. She nodded sadly. Once the announcement was made, she realized, there was no chance that the incident would turn out to be a dream or a hoax.

John Lennon was really dead.

"We had planned on so much," she'd tell the *New York Post.* "We had talked about living until we were eighty. We even drew up lists of all the things we could do together for all those years. Then, it was all over."

■ ■ ■

Geffen Records president Ed Rosenblatt called his boss, David Geffen, and told him that John Lennon had been shot. Geffen rushed to Roosevelt Hospital and somehow forced his way in. He found Yoko all by herself and led her out of the hospital.

A crowd had already gathered. Two college-age fans kneeled on the pavement, vowing to say the rosary until sunrise. In 1980, there were no barricades or publicists to control the media in this kind of situation; a celebrity had never been gunned down by a stalker.

Once Yoko arrived home, Dr. Lynn confirmed what the press already suspected. "I did tell his wife that he was dead," Lynn said, "and she was most distraught at the time, and found it hard to accept."

The NYPD anticipated that a few fans might gather in front of the Dakota. To control the small crowd, two police cars were stationed in the entranceway.

Mayor Koch was quick to issue a statement:

> John Lennon profoundly affected a generation. . . . He was an international figure, and New York City became his home. That made us very proud. Every death by violence is a trauma to society. The death of someone of John Lennon's stature intensifies this trauma. We mourn his loss.

Three decades later, Koch would remember his astonishment over the murder of John Lennon: "I liked the Beatles. I thought they were marvelous, sort of representative of our age, no matter how old or young we were. I was simply shocked that this could happen here in New York City."

15

HARD TO GO BACK AFTER THAT NEWSFLASH

At the Dakota, Yoko asked Geffen to inform Aunt Mimi, Julian, and the other Beatles.

Geffen couldn't find Ringo, but he managed to track down the drummer's secretary, Joan Woodgate. Joan called Ringo in the Bahamas. He and Barbara Bach had been drinking all day, and it took him a few seconds to focus. Was Joan saying that John was dead—that somebody had killed him? Ringo's heart pounded. He had to get to New York to be with Yoko.

Before he made the arrangements, though, he called his ex-wife, Maureen. Maureen had been part of the early Liverpool days with the Beatles. Ringo knew she'd feel the loss profoundly. As fate would have it, Cynthia Lennon happened to be asleep in her friend Maureen's home. She awoke to her friend's wails. Maureen placed Cynthia on the phone with Ringo. For a moment, it felt like 1963 again—Maureen, Cyn, and Ringo all together. Everybody loved John.

Except now everybody was crying.

■ ■ ■

For the past few months, seventeen-year-old Julian had been practicing guitar and drums, anticipating a visit with John after Christmas. It was the trip John had envisioned. Sean would be there, along with Aunt Mimi. "He was looking to his father for guidance," Cynthia said of her son in a public statement. "We don't know what will happen now."

Cynthia saw many of the traits John exhibited as a young man in Julian, including his haphazard wardrobe choices. Despite her initial hurt over the divorce, "everything has calmed down," she told writer Kate Shelley. "We talk on the phone. There's a much better understanding between us."

Indeed, Cynthia believed that *Double Fantasy* showed the true evolution of her ex-husband. "All that aggression is gone," she said. "I think it's super."

Likewise, communication between Julian and John had improved—they now spoke as frequently as three times a week. The bond needed strengthening, but Cynthia expected it to develop as Julian grew into an adult—with his own career as a musician.

Cynthia drove back to her home in Wales and told Julian about the murder. The teen asked to fly to New York to mourn with Sean and Yoko. Cynthia phoned the Dakota and spoke with her former adversary. Yoko made sure that Julian was booked on the next possible flight.

On television, CBS anchor Walter Cronkite broke into the network's regularly scheduled programming to tell Americans the news.

On NBC, a comedy sketch on *The Tonight Show Starring Johnny Carson* was interrupted by a slide containing the company logo, and an anonymous voice announcing the murder.

On ABC, the Miami Dolphins were playing the New England Patriots on *Monday Night Football*. Oddly, John had once been a guest on the show. In 1973 he was briefly interviewed by Howard Cosell and, while pleading ignorance of the rules of the game, said that American football "makes rock concerts look like tea parties." He'd consider a Beatles reunion, he joked, surveying the stadium, "if it looked like this." On the same show, then California Governor Ronald Reagan also made an appearance, and even explained the rules of the game to John off camera.

Today, however, there was no ironic celebrity chitchat. With the entire country listening, Cosell's colleague Frank Gifford flatly stated, "I don't care what's on the line, Howard. You have got to say what we know in the booth."

"Yes, we have to say it," a somber Cosell concurred.

"Remember, this is just a football game, no matter who wins or loses. An unspeakable tragedy, confirmed to us by ABC News in New York City. John Lennon, outside of his apartment building on the West Side of New York City, the most famous perhaps, of all the Beatles, shot...in the back." There was drama in his voice, something like the sorrow he'd exhibited during a 1977 World Series game, when cameras showed a fire raging near Yankee Stadium.

"There it is, ladies and gentlemen," he'd intoned, "the Bronx is burning."

At the time, the Brooklyn-raised commentator seemed appalled that a portion of the city he loved was being devoured by arsonists. Here, on December 8, 1980, he was aghast that Manhattan was the stage for a killer stepping from the shadows to slay a musical deity.

"Hard to go back to the game after that newsflash," Cosell recalled.

It was never easy being a sportscaster in New York City.

■   ■   ■

Graham Nash was home in bed, watching the football game. He and Lennon knew each other well. Even more upsetting than the murder, Nash would later say, was the thought of all the great material John would never get to write.

■   ■   ■

Nineteen-year-old bartender Adam Shanker also heard the *Monday Night Football* announcement, hanging out on the couch with his roommates in his apartment in New Rochelle. "I'd never experienced death like that before," Adam recalled. "We were all in a state of shock. It was so senseless that such a beautiful person who sang for peace and love could be cut down, just as he was singing about starting over."

Adam stood and reached for his coat. He was going back to Manhattan.

He presumed that at least a couple of like-minded souls would also be at the Dakota.

■ ■ ■

Disbelief swept through the building. Ten years earlier, as the city unraveled in racial strife and urban decay, the doorman had been stabbed to death by a mugger. But now—four years or so before the start of the city's crack era—the affluent residents were imbued with what turned out to be a false sense of security. Conductor Leonard Bernstein was said to be in a "state of shock" over the killing of the neighbor he'd called "Saint John."

In Sarasota, Florida, George Harrison's sister, Louise, had just gone to sleep when she was jolted awake by a phone call from a friend.

"Turn on the TV," the voice said cryptically.

Louise was worried that something had happened to George. Instead, she watched the story of John's murder with disbelief.

George didn't like to be bothered at home, and deliberately kept his phone under the stairs to avoid intrusions from the outside world. Louise rang and rang her brother. But no one picked up. After two hours, she called their brother, Harry, who—along with another sibling, Peter—worked as a groundskeeper at the former Beatle's Gothic estate in Henley-on-Thames, a onetime nunnery thirty-five miles from London.

Harry could read his brother's moods as well as anyone. George was asleep in the fifteen-bedroom mansion and wouldn't want to be woken up with such upsetting news. For the past several years, he'd attempted to live austerely in opulent surroundings, spending hours gardening his thirty-seven acres, adorned with gargoyles, turrets, and secret tunnels leading to underground lakes. Over time, George crafted giant arches from trees, and planted more than 400 maples.

George would learn about John's death soon enough, Harry reckoned. When George was finished with breakfast the next morning, Harry vowed to tell his brother everything. It wouldn't be easy—he was the one Beatle who hadn't fully made peace with John.

■　■　■

At the Waldorf-Astoria, reporters from all over the world listened raptly to every word President-elect Reagan uttered, trying to get a sense of the man who promised both to wield a big stick and to bring levity and glamour to an office currently mired in frustration over the Iranian hostage crisis. As the event wound down, the press corps was shaken by the news about John Lennon. Some stuck around to call in their notes or file their stories. A substantial number were instantly reassigned and dispatched to the 20th Precinct for Chief of Detectives James Sullivan's press conference.

Sullivan revealed the name of Lennon's attacker—and the fact that he'd been following the rock star around for days: "He was there on Saturday, asking about Mr. Lennon. He was there on Sunday, asking about Mr. Lennon. And he was there again this afternoon."

"It's an old rule," Sullivan said. "You become as famous as the guy you kill. From now on, any time there's something with the name Lennon, it's got to have the name Chapman with it. This kind of killing brings names closer together than marriage."

In Honolulu, reporters began to banging on Gloria Chapman's door. She refused to speak, saying only that her husband was "out of town."

A neighbor came to her aid. "Mrs. Chapman cannot come to the door now," the media was sharply told. "Questions will have to wait until tomorrow. She's distraught. Her health is in danger."

She spent the night calling the NYPD, desperately trying to learn more.

■ ■ ■

At WNEW-FM, disc jockey Vin Scelsa noticed that every light was glowing on the switchboard. He was confused. It was a Monday night, and he hadn't announced a giveaway. The mystery was cleared when a distraught desk assistant named Marty Martinez walked into the studio.

"John Lennon's been shot."

Scelsa had been playing Bruce Springsteen's "Jungleland," a nine-minute and thirty-three-second epic about love and violence. The deejay faded the music and read the bulletin, praying that John would survive. A short time later, Marty was back in the studio. As soon as Scelsa saw the tears, he knew that the rock legend had died.

"I didn't want to go on the air and say this," he later told MSNBC.com. "I knew right away that this was something that went beyond...a pop star death. This was truly a significant moment in our cultural history."

Like Walter Cronkite, who'd had the unfortunate burden of announcing John F. Kennedy's murder, Scelsa now addressed his constituency with tears dribbling down his cheeks.

Then he played "Let It Be."

From Long Island to central Jersey, Scelsa's listeners began leaving their homes for the Dakota.

■ ■ ■

"Cousin" Ken Dashow had only one stop left. Once he dropped off the heat blankets that had been used to keep the gear warm, he'd take the van home to Brooklyn. It was late, and he wasn't in the mood to ride the subway all the way out to Sheepshead Bay. The production company said he could return the vehicle in the morning.

Just before the Brooklyn Bridge, on Chambers Street, Vin Scelsa broke into the broadcast on WNEW. Ken was listening. He cut the wheel sharply to the right and pulled up on the sidewalk by City Hall. He had to compose himself.

Ken barely remembers the ride down the Brooklyn-Queens Expressway and up the Belt Parkway. At home, he poured himself a drink and listened to WNEW for the rest of the night.

"Little by little, all the deejays came into the station," he remembered. "It was just an all-night vigil on the air. As tired as I was, I stayed awake so I could share it with all the other Beatles fans."

Finally he grasped the reason why traffic had been diverted near Central Park.

■   ■   ■

After the Christmas tree lighting at Rockefeller Center, Paul LaRosa had dropped off his younger siblings and headed back to Queens, preparing for the lobster shift at the *Daily News*. At about 11:00 P.M., he was called and told to get to the Dakota immediately. For the second time that day, he drove toward Manhattan, listening to WNEW. The highway was virtually empty. He flew over the Triborough Bridge and down the FDR Drive, exiting at 110th Street in Spanish Harlem.

He hit Central Park, crossing Park Drive toward the West Side, when "Jungleland" came on the radio. "It was the perfect song for how everybody felt at that moment," Paul said. "I remember moaning along with Bruce in the car. It wasn't funny then. It was terrible. It was horrible. I felt a big hole in my soul. It was unheard of for a musician to be assassinated. I couldn't make sense of it. Who would shoot John Lennon?"

He grabbed a parking spot by the Dakota and walked over to the building. "There weren't a million police or horses all over the place," he said. "I remember the doorman and a few cops. The crowd was in the dozens, I'd say. Someone had whipped out a guitar and was singing 'Give Peace a Chance.'"

La Rosa concentrated on getting quotes. Then, he took a walk around the neighborhood, glumly noting the signed photos of John in the dry cleaners and diner.

Some one hundred miles from the Dakota, in Philadelphia, Bruce Springsteen sang "Tenth Avenue Freeze-Out," leaping across the stage, bending backward and sliding on his knees. Since October he'd been on the road, promoting his album *The River*, with a work ethic that would become legendary.

Neither Bruce nor any member of his E Street Band had any awareness of the role the song "Jungleland" was already playing in the John Lennon mythology. But as they walked down the ramp at the end of the concert, a member of the tech crew told them that John had been killed.

Drummer Max Weinberg was certain it was some sort of accident. When he learned the whole story, Weinberg said "it was just like all the air was sucked" out of the noisy arena.

■ ■ ■

In California, Stevie Wonder was told about the murder before going back on stage for an encore. He decided to perform the tune "Happy Birthday." The song had been written to advocate a national holiday in honor of Dr. Martin Luther King, Jr. But tonight, Stevie told his audience, he was singing for his friend, John: "We know that love can win / Let it out, don't hold it in."

■ ■ ■

In Paris, Mick Jagger was too "shattered" to speak at length. He thought about those recent visits to the Dakota, and was saddened that John had never come out of his living quarters to hang out. It would have been nice to spend a little more time with him.

"I knew and liked John Lennon for eighteen years," Jagger said. "But I don't want to make a casual remark now at such an awful time for his family, millions of fans and friends."

■ ■ ■

Ronni Katz stared at the television in her basement apartment in Flushing, Queens—walking distance, practically, from Shea Stadium. Sixteen years earlier, Ronni had been one of those teenage girls at Shea, screaming for the Beatles. And, like Chapman, she'd trailed her idols, shouting the names of the various band members in front of the Beatles' hotel. Ronni and her childhood friend Mary Faherty had seen *A Hard Day's Night* more than twenty-five times. They could even recite the first few lines with what they deemed were authentic Liverpudlian accents:

"Pardon me for asking. But who's that little old man?"
"What little old man?"
"That little old man."
"Oh, that one. That's my grandfather."

Now, Mary's mother called her daughter's old pal. "I am so sorry, dear," she told Ronni. "I know what it feels like to lose your first love."

■　■　■

Evan Ginzburg also lived in Flushing but had spent the night in Manhattan, at the wrestling matches at Madison Square Garden. "My father had died just a few months earlier, and I was in a fog anyway," he said. "There were no cell phones or pagers back then, but I just felt a very strange vibe, an eerie, disturbing feeling, when I walked out of the building.

"I knew something was wrong."

As the wrestling crowd intermingled with people on the street, Evan heard snippets of conversation—"John," "Lennon," "shot," and "murder." By the time he stepped onto the subway, he knew exactly what had occurred.

After he checked into the Ramada Inn on Forty-eighth and Eighth, Rick Martel realized that he'd been in the ring—with Tony Garea and the Wild Samoans—at the precise moment that Lennon was killed. There was a strange silence in the hotel bar. At the time, wrestling's good guys and bad guys kept their distance from each other in public. In-the-ring enemies never drank together.

The Wild Samoans were at the bar, along with bad guys The Moondogs, Rene Goulet, The Unpredictable Johnny Rodz, Larry Zbyszko, and some others. Afa nodded at Martel when he entered, and came over to him—right in front of the fans.

"You hear what happened to John Lennon?"

Martel looked up at the television screen. Sika slid over next to him, along with some fans. For one night, the rules had been waived.

■　■　■

Everyone Paul LaRosa interviewed for his article told essentially the same story: being drawn to the Dakota by forces too powerful to resist.

"There are Beatles songs I connect with every important event in my life," said a woman named Donna Samuelson, clutching a two-record set of recently released Beatles love songs. "Now, for the rest of my life, I'll think of this whenever I hear any of those songs, or remember any of those events."

Noted seventeen-year-old George Mamlouk, "Everybody talked about the Beatles getting back together again. Well, it won't happen now."

Paul wanted his story to contain more power than anything he'd written before. "I wanted it to be special," he said, "to make it equal the love I had for the Beatles, and what they meant to my life."

He worked feverishly, constantly searching for a pay phone the rest of the media hadn't discovered. His goal was avoiding an experience he'd had at the Metropolitan Opera after a bomb scare. As Paul called in his notes that day, women in furs pounded on the door of the phone booth.

"They were so pissed off at me—it was the only phone booth in the building," he said.

At a certain point, *Daily News* editor Bob Herbert—later a columnist for the *New York Times*—joined him outside the Dakota. Bob happened to live a block away, up Seventy-second Street. For the next several hours, the pair took turns visiting Bob's apartment and phoning in their notes.

Meanwhile, Paul Goresh was calling the city's dailies. In his camera, Goresh said, was a photo of John Lennon and his killer. But the newsrooms were frenzied, and few had patience for the Beatles fan from New Jersey.

At the *News*, Goresh got a veteran on the line. "What the fuck do you want?" the man barked. "Speak to me. What do you want?"

As Goresh stumbled, the man slammed down the receiver.

The photographer called the *Post*. No one there wanted to talk to him, either.

He called back the *News*.

This time, a reporter named Bob Lane sensed that Paul had something important to say. Lane was amazed by Goresh's story and believed every word. "Stay where you are," Lane urged. "Tell me where you live. I'll come and pick it up."

Grabbing some money from petty cash, Lane arranged for a car service to take him out to North Arlington, New Jersey. Then he and Goresh came back to the *Daily News* and went into the dark room.

"This is him," Paul said, watching the picture of Chapman and Lennon develop.

A deal was cut on the spot. The *Daily News* generally paid for tips. If something was good enough to land on Page Three, a reader could earn as much as fifty dollars.

This would be worth a bit more.

■　■　■

It was a good night for overtime at the 20th Precinct.

Cops had gone through Chapman's pockets, locating his Hawaiian gun permit and $2,200 in spending money. At 2:00 A.M., he sat across from detectives, freely offering insights into his worldview. There was the tale about his suicide attempt in Hawaii, and the voice that told him to kill.

"I just kept on hearing it," he explained.

"We got a psycho," one investigator commented to another.

Chapman wanted to talk more. "I've got a good side and bad side. The bad side is small but sometimes it takes over the good side, and I do bad things."

He was asked why he decided to kill Lennon.

"What kind of question is that?" the suspect snapped. "There are weak men, and there are strong men."

He refused to say anything else.

■   ■   ■

As Chapman spoke, fans outside the Dakota looked up toward the Lennons' windows, hoping for a sign from Yoko. She didn't deliver one. She was exhausted, and hysterical. She needed to sleep.

So far, at least five hundred people had gathered, and cops were erecting barricades. The Dakota's gates, as well as a nearby tree, were decorated with hand-written poems, flowers, drawings, and banners. Vendors peddled wreaths of roses, carnations, Christmas poinsettias, and lilies of the valley. Tape players blared. Horns honked. Fans were singing Beatles songs—singing themselves hoarse, like they were droning the team anthem at an English football match.

Yoko understood the visitors' positive intentions, but their behavior made it impossible to rest.

All she wanted was a little bit of peace on the worst night of her life.

Yoko summoned an assistant: "Can you please tell the people downstairs that I can't sleep?"

The assistant took the elevator downstairs and spoke to members of the crowd. They were sorry. They'd try to be quiet.

On this night, everyone loved Yoko. No one wanted to add to her desolation. Indeed, a single candle placed at the foot of the building's gate read, "For Yoko Ono."

The problem was that more fans kept arriving, and it was impossible to communicate the message to everyone. Within hours, the singing was even louder.

■　■　■

Dave Sholin's flight to San Francisco arrived late, but he was still excited by the three-hour interview with John and Yoko he had conducted at the Dakota earlier that day. In the car, he turned on KFRC, a Top 40 station where he'd worked as a disc jockey. There was a Beatles song on the radio. KFRC generally played more contemporary music, but the tune made Sholin smile, remembering the afternoon's conversation.

When the song ended, the deejay reminded listeners of the terrible news out of New York.

Dave could barely hold his hands on the wheel. He literally wondered whether he was having a nightmare.

At home, his phone rang all night. Every reporter in the country, it seemed, wanted to talk to the last journalist to interview John Lennon.

"It's a distinction I frankly wish wouldn't have happened," he'd later say.

■　■　■

At 6:20 A.M., Chapman was removed from the police precinct and driven to Manhattan Criminal Court. "We were afraid this guy would get assassinated," Cullen recounted, "so we had a little decoy at the stationhouse. We had someone else with a jacket over his head going out a side door, and Chapman went out the main door."

Cops never entertained the notion of placing Chapman with other prisoners. The suspect was locked in a six-by-eight-foot cell, where he paced before sitting in a corner and staring blindly ahead. After tiring of this, he flopped, face first, onto the bed, and started singing *Yellow Submarine*.

Oddly, he became annoyed when other prisoners taunted him with their own Beatles songs. Scrunching up his face, Chapman placed his hands over his ears in a fruitless effort to mute the commotion.

In another part of town, the man he'd killed was being transported from Roosevelt Hospital to the Chief Medical Examiner's Office for a forensic autopsy.

"John Lennon, we love you!" shouted a pedestrian.

It was 8:00 A.M. when Paul LaRosa called in the last of his notes. Then, he lingered in front of the Dakota and started singing with the crowd.

"Yes," he admitted. "I cried."

16

"DRAG, ISN'T IT?"

George Harrison, the Beatle who had preached compassion and nonviolence, could not contain his contempt for the man who killed his old friend. Despite the remarks Harrison had made about being held back by Lennon and McCartney, he was not immune to the pain. "After all we went through together," George said, "I had—and still have—great love and respect for" John.

In the ecosystem known as Planet Earth, George concluded, Chapman would be a parasite: "It is an outrage that people can take other people's lives when they obviously haven't got their own lives in order."

George was also beset by paranoia, worried about copycat killings and seeing every fan letter as a missive from a potential assassin. Even now, outside the estate, strangers were arriving to sing Beatles songs.

Their numbers were growing.

Just before he boarded his flight to New York, Ringo called Harrison. It was good to talk to someone who understood. Yoko called, as well. George offered her every condolence from the depths of his soul. Their conversation temporarily put him in a better mood. When it was over, George felt well enough to go into his home studio.

Al Kooper, a founding member of Blood, Sweat & Tears, had been playing and arranging songs on George's upcoming album. In the studio, Kooper, percussionist Ray Cooper, and John's old Liverpool friend Pete Shotton tried keeping George distracted, even plying the former Beatle with alcohol.

It didn't really work.

■   ■   ■

Remarkably, a significant number of New Yorkers didn't know about the murder until they left their homes the next morning. Some hadn't watched the news; others went to bed early. On the way to work, though, everyone saw the covers of the city's tabloids.

The front page of the *Daily News* contained a large photo of David Geffen leading Yoko Ono through a crowd. Above it was the headline:

JOHN LENNON SLAIN HERE

To the left of the photo was a smaller picture of John, above the words

Killed outside his apartment

Inside was a quote from Nina McFadden, an Upper West Side resident who'd been passing by the Dakota when the gun was fired. "I saw John and Yoko step out of the limousine," she said. "They walked inside the gate. Then I heard four or five shots. They were ear-splitting.

"I heard Yoko scream, 'Help him. Help him.' It was then that I saw the man with the gun."

Barbara Tyree, a nanny caring for two children on the Dakota's ground floor, recalled looking out the family's window to behold a scene of turbulence and confusion. "It was terrible," she said. "Terrible."

The *New York Post* carried George Arzt's quotes from Ellen Chesler. "It's very, very tragic," she told the paper. "To the rest of the world, it's John Lennon, but if you live in the building, it's a neighbor."

At City Hall, Mayor Ed Koch read the article, then summoned Ellen, whose office was just at the opposite end of the corridor. Deputy Mayor Bob Wagner, Jr., was also in the room.

"He was so amazed by this whole thing," Ellen said of the mayor. "This was an international tragedy and I was an eyewitness. I was the celebrity of the day."

■ ■ ■

Karen Becker had spent the night listening to WPLJ in New York and speaking to her brother, Dave, on the phone about John's murder. She'd wanted to join the people outside the Dakota, but for the last three years, she'd been a school teacher—a genuine adult—and had a classroom of students to teach at a Greek Orthodox school in Astoria, Queens, first thing in the morning.

"I went to work in the morning," she said. "It was surreal. A part of me felt like I had died with John Lennon. The only way I could think to show I was mourning was to wear a black armband into the classroom."

The assistant principal spotted it, as Karen walked into the building. He looked at her sympathetically.

"I guess that means we have to grow up now."

■ ■ ■

Chapman sounded coherent as he spoke to Gloria on the phone. Having elevated his status from that of a nobody, Mark had regained the capacity to consider the needs of others. "Hire a lawyer," he counseled. "You have to protect yourself."

She followed this simple instruction. The attorney, Brook Hart, immediately rejected financial offers from those wishing to publish Gloria's memoirs, emphasizing that she'd always been a private person and would never profit from the tragedy.

Asked about the theory that Chapman had killed because he believed that he was the real John Lennon, Hart replied, "Those assertions are likely to have a great deal of truth."

At a press conference, Gloria showed complete contrition— so much so that even the most hardened reporters in the room appeared sensitive to her predicament.

She claimed that she was "very sorry this had to happen, that John Lennon had to die, and his wife and son had to suffer. I also mourn the death of John Lennon."

Yet the Christian convert believed deeply in forgiveness. She'd always absolved Mark, she explained, "when he did things in the past."

Her message to her troubled husband: "I love you."

■ ■ ■

Like George, Paul McCartney avoided the telephone. At night at their country home, Paul and Linda preferred interacting with their children to watching television or even listening to the radio. On the morning of December 9, while Linda was driving the kids to school, Paul plugged in the phone. The first caller told him everything that he needed to know.

Even the death of his mother hadn't hit him this hard.

At least he'd been ready for that.

He felt fury, sadness, fear. All he'd ever wanted to do was play music, and make people happy. His 1976 tune, "Silly Love Songs"—a slap at Lennon for diminishing Paul's penchant for "silly love songs"—expressed his philosophy: "Some people wanna fill the world with silly love songs / And what's wrong with that?"

Now, there were killers out there, not only watching him, but maybe his wife and children. When Linda returned, Paul was a mess, shaking and weeping.

He called George—two men mourning the loss of a brother. He called Yoko. The relationship with John had been so intense. Sometimes John was a jerk, sometimes he put Paul in his place. Yoko told Paul that John had never stopped loving his bandmate. Paul spoke about his affection for John. But he also comforted Yoko, who still couldn't understand why anyone would take John away from his family.

Neither could Paul.

He'd always worried about Julian. Now he was heartbroken for Sean.

He had to do something to remedy the pain. Otherwise, he felt like he'd have a complete breakdown. When George Martin called, Paul said that he and Linda would be coming into the studio. Maybe he could channel his feelings into the music.

The couple got into their limousine and drove up to where the media were gathered. The cameras caught an ashen man. "I can't take it in at the moment," Paul said. "John was a great guy. He is going to be missed by the whole world."

The vehicle lurched forward. Paul knew there'd be more reporters at the studio. In fact, the press was probably going to follow him around for days. He and Linda discussed attending John's funeral. They couldn't do it. Paul's presence would cause bedlam. John didn't deserve such an undignified end. His warmth, his transformation to family man, even his lack of moderation—those were the things that people needed to remember, not the sight of the paparazzi chasing Paul McCartney. Yoko knew that Paul cared—that's what was important.

Still, he wanted to underscore his sentiments.

When he addressed the next media horde, he'd encourage "everyone to rally around Yoko."

■   ■   ■

Ringo stepped out of the limousine on West Seventy-second Street, his hair rumpled, his eyes red. Despite the time he'd spent in the tropical sun, his skin was practically white. He'd come to support Yoko, but his arrival seemed to inflame the tragedy. Fans swarmed him from all directions. Observers stood on cars and shouted.

"Give him space!" someone yelled.

A group of Dakota employees attempted to form an impromptu security detail around the drummer. But they could only do so much. Someone jammed a shoulder into the weary ex-Beatle, and Ringo's head snapped backward. He closed his eyes for a moment, then attempted to move forward. One woman reached over and grabbed his hair. This kind of thing had happened during Beatle-mania, but now? Ringo shook the hand free and looked at the woman, confused. But he opted not to say anything.

He was there for John's family, not for himself.

John's old friend embraced and talked with Yoko for two hours. Of all the Beatles, he'd always been the most accepting of the woman John chose as his life partner, and Yoko liked him without qualifications.

The crowd had gotten bigger by the time Ringo departed, chasing after his limo as it rolled away from the Dakota, toward the airport. Ringo was going to L.A. It certainly wasn't going to help Yoko to have fans following a Beatle all over New York.

Plus, Ringo wasn't feeling particularly fond of the city where his buddy had been killed.

■　■　■

After Ringo left, Yoko's body literally ached with pain. She called for John out of habit, and realized that he was no longer there.

She issued a statement that there would be no funeral for her husband; the scene outside the Dakota was chaotic enough. "John loved and prayed for the human race," she said. "Please do the same for him."

Sean had been insulated from the murder—until Yoko called him into her bedroom. The five-year-old could see that his mother was sad, and asked for his father. Although the child was unaware of what had transpired on the sidewalk downstairs, he could sense that John was gone. Yoko confirmed this.

"Your father's dead."

She showed him the newspaper to substantiate what neither wanted to believe.

Yoko took her son by the hand and led him downstairs to the spot where his father had collapsed. Neighbors and workers at the Dakota stepped out of the way, wiping their eyes as the boy studied the floor.

Yoko attempted to explain the notion of a deranged fan killing his idol.

Sean had difficulty comprehending this. "If you like someone, why would you hurt him?"

"This was a very confused person."

Sean attempted to digest the information. "We should find out if he was really confused or if he really had meant to kill him."

"That's up to the court."

"A court? Like a tennis court or a basketball court?"

Sean's question cheered Yoko. She thought about the way John and his little boy talked and played, zoning in on one word and building a conversation around it.

"Now Daddy is a part of God," Sean said. "I guess when you die, you become much more bigger because you're part of everything."

The pair returned upstairs. The child didn't want his mother to see him cry. He went to his room and tried writing a poem with watery eyes. Finally, he understood why so many strangers were massing around his home. "I remember the sound of the people outside," he'd tell *New York* magazine three decades later, "the fires and the singing the songs and the police tape downstairs, *Double Fantasy* being recorded, my dad's voice, the texture of his skin, the look of his ankle. It's like I awoke from a dream, and I've never been a child since then."

■　■　■

At the Knickerbocker Pub, Adam Shanker could barely serve drinks. "I was a wreck, working at the bar," he remembered. "I was crying at work, and people understood. The whole city was in a state of shock."

■　■　■

Todd Rundgren tried absorbing reports that his work had become immensely appealing to Mark David Chapman—due to "Rock and Roll Pussy" and the perceived feud with John Lennon. "I recognize it as one of life's unfortunate occurrences," he said of the inclusion of *The Battle of Todd Rundgren* on the shrine Chapman left behind at the Sheraton. As a rock star, Rundgren was realistic, and knew that his followers included a smattering of less than stable devotees.

"You're just lucky that you don't meet them most of the time," he'd tell *Spinner*.

In Washington, President Jimmy Carter praised John's "spirit—the spirit of the Beatles—brash and earnest, ironic and idealistic all at once." As someone who aspired to many of the same ideals, Carter claimed to be "distressed by the senseless manner" in which the former Beatle was killed. "It is especially poignant that John Lennon has died by violence, though he had long campaigned for peace."

President-elect Reagan was ending a meeting with Terence Cardinal Cooke when reporters asked about the slain Beatle. "What can anyone say?" Reagan replied, fumbling for words. "It's a great tragedy. It's just another evidence . . . that we have to try to stop tragedies of this sort."

As Cooke listened, Reagan expounded, "The whole overall picture of violence in our streets has got to be treated with, and we have to find an answer." Nonetheless, the conservative, former governor of California, stressed that gun control was not the solution.

"I've never believed that," he told reporters, as the Cardinal very subtly stepped away from the future commander-in-chief. "I believe in the kind of handgun legislation we had in California. . . . If somebody commits a crime and carries a gun when he's doing it, add five to fifteen years to the prison sentence."

The proposition did nothing to moderate the concerns of Yoko's brother, Keisuke. From Tokyo, he blamed the death directly on American gun culture and urged Yoko to relocate to the nation of her birth—a place, Keisuke maintained, "where she doesn't have to worry about gunshots anymore."

But Yoko wasn't leaving New York—a city very different from the America that had elected Ronald Reagan and shared his commitment to the right to bear arms. "There ought not to be the opportunity to purchase handguns anywhere in the U.S.," Mayor Koch told reporters.

Nonetheless, he bristled at condemnations of the city from abroad, particularly the UK, where London's *New Standard* editorialized that John's "meaningless murder is increasingly typical of New York and the United States in general, where the freedom to carry guns has brought forth monsters."

"Are there no monsters in Britain?" Koch countered, sounding very much like John Lennon. "Ask the people of Ireland."

■　■　■

At 3:10 P.M., Chapman was led out of his cell at Manhattan Criminal Court and into Room 129 for his arraignment. The courtroom was packed, with every observer studying the suspect's expression. Three years earlier, when David Berkowitz was revealed as the "Son of Sam"—the mysterious assailant who randomly murdered six New Yorkers and wounded another seven—he'd smiled in custody and taunted a victim's mother in the courtroom. There was none of this in Chapman. He neither grinned nor grimaced. Those who managed to look into his face saw nothing.

Chapman was charged with murder in the second degree—as were all capital defendants in New York State, since a first-degree conviction meant a possible death sentence. As he listened to Assistant District Attorney Kim Hogrefe tell the court that he "deliberately premeditated execution of John Lennon," Chapman dipped his head forward.

His court appointed attorney, Herbert Adlerberg, stressed that Mark heard voices and was convinced that Satan influenced his actions. As a result, the lawyer said, his client was "not fully cognizant of what is going on," and his team would mount an insanity defense.

■ ■ ■

While the BBC was running the movie *Help* as part of its tribute to Lennon, in the United States, television news viewers repeatedly listened to the depiction of John's murder, with each on-air personality attempting to frame Chapman's irrational actions in a context that appealed to common sense. Alan Weiss's station, WABC in New York, showed images of Chapman being led into custody with a coat over his head. Iconic anchor Roger Grimsby portrayed the suspect as a ne'er-do-well whose inability to hold a job may have led to the eruption in front of the Dakota.

"Good evening, I'm Roger Grimsby," the newsman intoned at the start of the dinnertime broadcast, "Mark David Chapman, twenty-five years of age, a former security guard, now unemployed and now accused of murder."

The cameras then flashed back to the events of less than twenty-four hours before, showing a panic-stricken witness in front of the Dakota.

"Who got shot?" the woman was asked.

"John Lennon."

Lennon's producer Jack Douglas was also seen running into Roosevelt Hospital. "Please tell someone I'm here," he was heard saying. "He just left me five minutes before."

On the CBS network, anchor Charles Osgood spoke to a national audience about the world's surprise over the attack, as well as the collective bereavement:

> Last night, in the courtyard of the landmarked New York City building where he lived, John Lennon was shot to death. . . . His assailant was a perfect stranger. It happened so suddenly, so senselessly that there was no time . . . to run and hide. . . . The world . . . is grieving over John Lennon as if he'd been a world leader, a king or a president. Not many kings or presidents are mourned this much.

■ ■ ■

John's half-sister Julia Baird refused to watch television, unable to abide the agitated voices of witnesses, the detached legalese from authorities, and the images of John and his family so happy in New York. She wanted to know details, however, and was willing to read the newspaper, since it allowed her to control the flow of information to her brain. If a passage was particularly disturbing, she could turn the page or put away the paper until her nerves calmed.

At AIR Studios in London, Paul and George Martin literally cried on one another. Although Paul spent part of the day attempting to make music, much of the time consisted of the two telling entertaining tales about a fallen friend, as if they were at a wake.

When Paul stepped back out onto Oxford Street, the reporters were waiting. He was physically drained from crying, and the tears weren't over yet. Chewing gum, he half-listened as questions flew from every direction. "I was very shocked, you know," he responded to perhaps the fiftieth inquiry he'd heard that day about his reaction. "This is terrible news."

He'd come to the studio, he stated, because he "just didn't want to sit at home."

"Why?" someone asked.

"I didn't feel like it."

A reporter wanted to know when he learned of the murder.

"The morning sometime."

"Very early?"

"Yeah."

Under these circumstances, the most sensible comment Paul could dispense was, "Drag, isn't it?"

He stepped back into the limo, thinking not about his remark, but John. It wasn't until the image of Paul muttering "drag" played all over the world that he grasped his poor choice of words.

To a public that knew nothing of Paul's visits to the Dakota and the discussions about a Beatles reunion in Central Park, Paul and John were still enemies. When Paul walked out of the studio, it looked like he'd gone to work, as if it were a normal day. The "just didn't want to sit home" comment appeared reminiscent of a Beatles press conference, Paul throwing out the obvious for his own amusement.

The gum-chewing seemed to indicate indifference.

"Drag, isn't it?" came off as dismissive of the journalists who wanted to hear something deep and heartfelt.

That Paul had praised John during previous media encounters that day mattered little. The "drag" statement was the one that played on every newscast from Hong Kong to Tipperary. At least he'd spoken to Yoko first; John's family knew how Paul really felt. But he didn't want to be perceived as something he was not. He'd later clarify his frame of mind, maintaining that he'd meant no disrespect whatsoever.

On the evening of December 9, though, Paul was done granting interviews. With his children, he sat in front of the television set, watching the news, unable to control his tears.

■　■　■

At the Dakota, Julian Lennon emerged from a limo. There was more security around the building since Ringo departed, and fans kept their hands to themselves. The teenager said nothing as he was led upstairs.

"Who's that?" came a voice in the crowd.

"Julian."

The next time he came outside, no one had to ask about his identity. Fans chanted his name over and over, holding up photos of the father who'd endowed him with his looks, musical ability— and emotional issues yet to be resolved.

■　■　■

For the second straight night, Bruce Springsteen and the E Street Band took the stage in Philadelphia. There'd been dissension in the band over this. Guitarist "Miami Steve" Van Zandt lobbied for taking the night off in honor of Lennon. Bruce insisted that the show must go on. And, in front of the crowd, he explained why: "It's a hard world that asks you to live with a lot of things that are unlivable. And it's hard to come out here and play tonight, but there's nothing else we can do."

Like the Beatles, Springsteen believed that the E Street Band members were musicians who had a special obligation to the fans who'd waited for tickets and altered their schedules to see the concert. He couldn't leave them flat. He opened the show with a possessed variation of his best-known song, "Born to Run," and ended the night with his own interpretation of "Twist and Shout."

■　■　■

Chapman was dispatched to the psychiatric ward at Bellevue for thirty days of evaluation while awaiting his next hearing. He spent the first night alone, in a cell containing four beds and a barred window, politely following instructions.

"He's not a screaming crazy," a hospital representative told the *New York Post*. "It was an uneventful night. Everything is really normal."

Nonetheless, a guard peeked in through the window of the large, bolted door every fifteen minutes. Given Chapman's history, authorities thought it was best to place to place him on twenty-four-hour suicide watch.

"We're really careful because of the nature of this," the spokesperson elaborated.

Of course, Chapman was already under analysis—from the public and the press. Psychologists courted the media, offering their characterization of the murder as a pathological replay of the ancient drama involving a son slaughtering a father to take his place.

"It's very possible that he saw himself as the leader of the Beatles," one therapist theorized to the *Daily News*. "The guy probably sat in his room, playing the guitar to Beatles records, and imagined himself on stage at Shea Stadium."

■ ■ ■

Inspired by images of New Yorkers paying tribute to Lennon, in California 2,000 Angelinos held a candlelit vigil in Century City.

At the Lincoln Memorial, several hundred engaged in a "silent tribute." In Cincinnati, 1,500 mourners were pelted by wind and freezing rain. A little further south, the Rev. Jesse Jackson led 3,000 primarily African-American fans in prayer in Chattanooga, Tennessee.

In Seattle, Tower Records reported customers walking through the door and purchasing two copies of *Double Fantasy* at a time. Back in New York, every album featuring John Lennon sold out at King Karol Records in Times Square, and employees at Geffen Records were called in to press more copies of *Double Fantasy*—after a reported one million orders were received.

"A popular album sells about fifty in a day, but this is incredible," a King Karol employee marveled. "We sold 200 copies of Lennon's latest album in one day."

At the Discomat III store on Broadway, 275 *Double Fantasy* albums were gone in an eleven-hour period. Said manager Bill Koenig, "The only time something like this happened before was when Elvis died. Many people came into the store crying."

Double Fantasy would become John Lennon's best-selling studio LP—and win a 1981 Grammy for Album of the Year—with three million shipments just in the United States. By in end of 1980, "(Just Like) Starting Over" was the #1 single in the country, replacing "Lady" by Kenny Rogers. In the UK the next month, the late Beatle would have an unprecedented three singles in the Top 5: "(Just Like) Starting Over," "Woman," and a reissued version of "Imagine."

■ ■ ■

Two days after John Lennon's murder, the Beatle was quietly cremated at Ferncliff Cemetery in Hartsdale, New York, just north of the Bronx. The ashes were given to Yoko, who made sure that they wouldn't be displayed in public, honoring her husband's disdain for the "cult worship" of dead musicians.

Yoko asked fans not to send flowers to the Dakota, but to contribute to the Spirit Foundation, the fund the couple founded in 1979 to avoid being solicited by a torrent of individual requests. Among the organizations the foundation supportered: Harlem Family Health Service, New York's public television station WNET, alternative radio outlet WBAI-FM, the Salvation Army and the Police Athletic League—reiterations that the affection New Yorkers felt for John and Yoko was reciprocated every day.

But Yoko was apprehensive about those fans who loved John a little too much. The day before the cremation, in Brooksville, Florida, Jean Costello had found the body of her sixteen-year-old daughter, Colleen, in the girl's bedroom. The teen had taken an overdose of pills. Colleen had been struggling with a number of issues, but, according to her mother, John's death was the "straw that broke the camel's back."

In Salt Lake City, thirty-year-old Michael Craig watched news reports of the murder and told a friend, "I think I'll end it all." He then raised a pistol to his mouth and fired, dying from a .25-caliber bullet wound.

Yoko wanted to grieve privately for John, but the news of the suicides so upset her that she called the *Daily News*, pleading with fans not to capitulate to their despondency over the murder.

"People are committing suicide," she said, her voice breaking. "They are sending me telegrams saying that this is the end of an era and everything. I'm really so concerned.... That sort of thinking is against what we believe in, and when something like this happens, each one of us must go on."

17

SORROW INTO CLARITY

It took Chapman's lawyer approximately one day to quit the case. Less than twenty-four hours after his arraignment, Chapman was woken up in Bellevue and outfitted with a bulletproof vest. Surrounded by a phalanx of officers, the suspect was led downstairs to First Avenue. The entire street had been closed to traffic. Two police vans and a number of cruisers were waiting. Chapman was placed in one of the vehicles—because of assassination fears, officials wouldn't specify which—before the procession moved to Manhattan Criminal Court for a surprise hearing.

As courthouse visitors were searched, scanned by metal detectors, and ordered to produce identification—rigorous security precautions for 1980—Chapman's attorney, Herbert Alderberg, entered the building, flanked on each side by a detective from the District Attorney's office. They'd been assigned to him after a flood of threatening phone calls to Alderberg's office.

In front of Judge Rena Uviller, Alderberg explained that callers had pledged to kill both him and his family if Chapman were acquitted. Since a defense attorney's mission was supposed to be securing a client's freedom, Alderberg argued that his preoccupation with his own safety would compromise his ability to defend Chapman.

By the afternoon, another lawyer had stepped in. Jonathan Marks, a former assistant U.S. attorney, was used to inciting the public. Earlier in the year—in another case that received daily media coverage—his vigorous defense of a man accused of shoving seventeen-year-old flutist Renee Katz in front of an oncoming subway train, severing her hand, had resulted in an acquittal.

■ ■ ■

As Yoko warned fans to refrain from thoughts of vigilantism—"this is not a time for hate or disillusionment"—she learned that the most unhinged members of society fantasized about exacerbating the tragedy. Outside the Dakota, police arrested a man who'd suddenly materialized, vowing to kill Yoko. This occurred after another disturbed male had turned up at Los Angeles International Airport, broadcasting his plan to murder Ringo as soon as his flight from New York landed.

Ringo would later observe that John's death brought out the worst in certain types of individuals: "It's like there were people out there who decided they wanted to get their own Beatle." While the comment sounded humorous, much of the rock community was genuinely terrified.

On December 11, the *New York Post* ran a front page photo—apparently taken by an attendant—of Lennon's body in the morgue, prior to his cremation. During the Son of Sam case, the *Daily News* had won the city's tabloid battles, thanks to killer David Berkowitz's decision to write directly to columnist Jimmy Breslin. The *Post's* Steve Dunleavy tried wresting away the crown, composing open letters to the serial killer. But Berkowitz was apparently too busy writing to Breslin to notice. This time around, the *Post* was determined not to get beaten. Although newspaper people understood this principle, musicians viewed the photo as a violation—and proof that, if someone was out to get you, even your own death couldn't stop them.

Within twenty-four hours of John's death, Paul had hired two guards to patrol the grounds of his estate and screen visitors—whether the McCartneys were there or not. The investment was apparently a wise one. In 1984, British police arrested several alleged conspirators said to be involved in a scheme to raid the home, kidnap Linda McCartney, and hold her for a $12.6 million ransom.

■ ■ ■

At Bellevue, officials remained concerned for Chapman's safety—from himself, as well as others. Responding to rumors that fans were plotting to storm the hospital, authorities revised their plan to hold the suspect there for thirty days. On December 12, he was transferred to a jail cell on Rikers Island, the 413-acre complex in the East River, between Queens and the Bronx.

There, the problems intensified. The Rikers inmates saw Chapman as a coward, and immediately bullied him, scrawling on a wall: "Champlain [sic], you have not much time laft [sic]. Don't feel pity. Now it is behind that point."

Although he was protected from physical contact with other prisoners, Chapman interpreted the message to mean that his food had already been poisoned. As a result, he went on a hunger strike. Not wishing to see their most notorious inmate whittle away before his trial, Rikers officials were forced to make some changes, moving about twenty inmates from an infirmary area in order to house Chapman there alone. There, in his seven-by-seven cell, he agreed to eat.

■ ■ ■

With each hour, the streets around the Dakota seemed to become more congested. "I've been coming here every day for practically the whole day," sixteen-year-old Annette Newman of Queens told the *Daily News*. "It's better if we're all together for this, rather than taking it alone. You have to be with people who know how you feel."

Even without a funeral, John's supporters needed a formal way to say goodbye, and Yoko and the city arranged for a special gathering in Central Park—a ten-minute "period of remembrance" on Sunday afternoon, December 14.

Approximately forty hardcores camped out in the park the night before, sharing their memories of John in the twenty-four-degree chill. When the sun came up, an estimated 100,000 people began to congregate. Florist Phillip Atlas stood on West Seventy-second Street, handing out 2,000 daisies. On the grass, between Seventy-first and Seventy-fourth Streets, fans held flowers and lit candles. For half an hour, Beatles music blasted from speakers on a rental truck. For the next thirty minutes, fans stood in contemplation while classical music played. Then, came the silence—a powerful, unanimous hush.

Bodies rubbed against each other. People closed their eyes or stared ahead, some praying, some thinking of John, his sad end, and his dream of peace. From the center of the crowd, the New York December felt warm, comfortable, maybe even a little mellow.

In Liverpool, 30,000 came together to venerate the audacious kid from the Quarry Bank Grammar School who'd become the rough northern city's most prolific voice. Around New York, there were spontaneous tributes. As Christmas shoppers bustled in and out of Macy's in Herald Square, a couple bowed their heads in the center of the sidewalk. In Grand Central Station, a group of teenagers circled around a radio playing Beatles songs, listening in stillness.

"Come together right now over me."

David Geffen read a message from Yoko: "Bless you for your tears and prayers. I saw John smiling in the sky. I saw sorrow changing into clarity. I saw all of us becoming one mind.

"Thank you."

■　■　■

Ken Dashow was working his weekend shift at WRCN Radio in Riverhead, Long Island, playing Beatles music and talking about Lennon. When the fans in Central Park meditated over John, Ken and his program director decided to go silent for a full minute.

"The worst thing that can happen in radio is silence," he said. "But I'll never forget—this was the loudest silence. No band ever played louder than that moment of silence."

■   ▣   ■

In Shayne's Circus of Values, in Lake Ronkonkoma, Long Island, two teen cashiers agreed to turn their backs on their registers and observe the ten minutes of silence.

"It was a matter of principle," seventeen-year-old Suzanne Stephens explained.

The customers at the discount store displayed little sympathy. "She stopped the store," a Shayne's spokesperson complained to the *Post*. "She told one customer, 'After the vigil'…People were yelling and screaming, and she acted like they weren't there. They were dropping the merchandise and walking out."

Because of this, the other cashier, eighteen-year-old Donna Palmieri, returned to the register after two minutes. She was given a reprimand after signing a letter of apology.

Suzanne, on the other hand, was fired.

"I would do it again," she told the newspaper. "It's something I believe in."

■   ■   ■

At the Bandshell in Central Park, Adam Shanker joined a group singing "Come Together," "Imagine," and "A Day in the Life." "We were all dealing with our emotions, but everyone in the crowd had feelings that were in harmony," he said. "As people were leaving Central Park, large snowflakes started to fall. I don't believe in higher powers, but I felt that the power of so many of our feelings created the falling flakes."

In the weeks that followed, Adam found it difficult to listen to *Double Fantasy*, and the whole process of hearing John's music became an entirely different experience. On Adam's wedding day in 1997, he walked down the aisle to "Grow Old with Me," a song originally slated for *Double Fantasy* and released posthumously, in 1984, on John and Yoko's *Milk and Honey* LP: "Grow old along with me," John says. "Two branches of one tree."

■   ■   ■

As fans were singing Beatles songs across the street from the Dakota, Ellen Chesler and her husband listened to the group's albums in the their apartment. "I don't think I had any of the originals," she said, "just the greatest hits records, the compilations."

Within the building, there was a great deal of concern for John's family—as well as for the safety of the residents. Everyone knew where the Lennons lived now, and that increased the likelihood of crazies appearing at the front gate.

18

WITH EVERY DROP THAT FALLS, WE HEAR YOUR NAME

At a January 1981 hearing, Mark David Chapman's attorney, Jonathan Marks, entered a plea of not guilty by reason of insanity. Nine mental health professionals were prepared to testify at the trial. Six would reinforce the defense's claim that the defendant was psychotic, and not liable for his actions. Three insisted that Chapman, while clearly delusional, was competent enough to be held accountable for the murder. Prosecutors were expected to argue that Chapman's inability to live in social harmony came from being a sociopath, a person whose lack of conscience and moral responsibility allowed him to justify his proclivity for violating the rights of others.

In February, Chapman wrote a letter to the *New York Times*, maintaining that he *was* concerned about his fellow citizens, and believed they could achieve a degree of enlightenment, if not salvation, by reading his favorite book.

"My wish is for all of you to someday read *The Catcher in the Rye*," he wrote. "All of my efforts will now be devoted toward this goal, for this extraordinary book holds many answers. My true hope is that in wanting to find these answers, you will read *The Catcher in the Rye*."

The message was signed, with ballpoint pen, "Mark David Chapman—The Catcher in the Rye."

Four months later, on June 22, 1981, Chapman sounded less grandiose when, against his lawyer's advice, he pleaded guilty to second-degree murder—saving Yoko the anguish of having to face her husband's killer in court, and depriving the tabloid press of the cavalcade of witnesses, VIP spectators, Beatles fans, and feuding jurors to interview.

Judge Dennis Edwards informed the defendant that his plea was equivalent to a guilty verdict.

"By waiving and giving up your right to a trial," Edwards said, "you give up your right... to either question the witnesses produced by the prosecution and produce witnesses in your behalf by the defense. Do you understand?"

"Yes, Your Honor," Chapman answered.

Edwards asked the defendant to tell the court exactly what had transpired on December 8, 1980.

"I intended to kill John Lennon," Chapman replied with clinical authority. "And that night, I drew a pistol from my pocket and proceeded to shoot him with intent to kill him."

"All right. Do you recall how many shots you fired from the pistol?"

"Five shots."

"...Do you know how many shots struck the victim?"

"Yes, Your Honor, I do."

"How many were there?"

"Four."

"...Would you tell us approximately how far away you were from the victim, Mr. Lennon, when you started to fire the shots?"

"I am not quite sure, but I think it is around twenty feet."

Chapman noted that John had been approaching the door to the Dakota's security area when "I stepped off the curb and walked a few steps over, turned, withdrew my pistol and aimed at him in his direction, and fired off five shots in quick succession."

Assistant District Attorney Allen Sullivan then asked Chapman about the types of bullets he used.

"They were .38 hollow-points."

"What was the reason for using hollow-points?"

"To ensure John Lennon's death."

The prosecutor inquired why Chapman had decided to plead guilty.

"It is my decision and God's decision."

"When you say it is God's decision…did you hear any voices in your ears?"

"Any audible voices?" Apparently, Chapman was trying to distinguish between these and the inner voice he claimed motivated him to kill.

"Any audible voices."

"No, sir."

The topic switched to the thought process behind the guilty plea. "Before you made this decision, did you indulge in any prayer?" Sullivan queried.

"Yes, there were a number of prayers."

"After you prayed, did you come to the realization which you understand came from God that you should plead guilty?"

"Yes, that is his directive, command.…Probing with my own decision whether to do what God wanted me to do…I decided to follow God's directive."

"So would you say at this time that this plea is a result of your own free will?"

"Yes."

Judge Edwards resumed questioning, asking Chapman if he'd been threatened into pleading guilty.

"No, Your Honor."

"Have any promises been made to compel you or induce you to plead guilty?"

"No, in such words. But I have been assured by God that wherever I go, he will take care of me."

"A good Christian ethic," the judge declared. "I presume we all feel that God will assist us in times of need and emergency."

Despite defense protestations, the court ruled that Chapman was competent enough to determine his future. No further assessments were necessary.

The guilty plea stood.

■   ■   ■

Manhattan's city councilman-at-large, Henry Stern, didn't anticipate a problem when he sponsored a resolution memorializing John Lennon's "genius." But the only Republican on the city council, Angelo Arculeo of Bay Ridge, Brooklyn, opposed the measure. Lennon, Arcuelo remembered, had been a drug user and a radical. Furthermore, the councilman proclaimed, he didn't "recall these types of tributes being extended to Bing Crosby, who really *was* an American legend."

Stern branded his fellow legislator a "blue meanie."

"The rules of the Council were that if anybody objected, the resolution would not be adopted," Stern recounted. "So the tribute was rejected."

Stern had much better luck in 1981, initiating legislation to label a section of Central Park, across from the Dakota, "Strawberry Fields." Stern's vision was relatively small. The Parks Department installed a Strawberry Fields marker; some bushes and trees were planted, and unsightly shrubbery was removed.

Then Yoko contacted the Central Park Conservancy—the non-profit organization that had recently begun managing the park—and offered to assist. "She ended up giving about $1-million," recalled Stern, the future Parks Commissioner.

"She wanted an international garden of peace, with plants from every country in the world. It was a wonderful idea. But plants from every country don't grow in this climate. It's just a fact of nature. Some people wanted literally strawberry fields, and they did plant strawberries there. I don't remember how they looked."

No matter, Strawberry Fields ended up becoming an exquisite haven of tranquility. At its core is a circular pathway of inlaid stones, a gift from the city of Naples. Bordered by benches, the center of the mosaic reads, "Imagine." From there, visitors can journey to numerous open and secret glades, containing rhododendrons, hollies, mountain laurel, wild shrub roses, and a collection of dawn redwood trees whose tops will eventually be visible from several blocks away. Over the years, fans have gathered at the location to mark the anniversary of John's murder, Beatle birthdays, the death of Grateful Dead guitarist Jerry Garcia, 9/11, and other occasions. To regulars there, one homeless man, Gary dos Santos, became almost as famous as the site, laying flowers and objects in the circular memorial in the shape of a peace sign.

His garnishments stimulated introspection in both strangers and those who'd managed to cross paths with John.

"Sometimes, when I walk through Strawberry Fields, I think, 'Imagine if I had been in a situation where I could have done something,'" Dr. Richard Marks, the emergency room surgeon at Roosevelt Hospital, told *People.* "'Imagine if the wounds were in a different place. Imagine if only he had been savable.'"

■ ■ ■

On the day Chapman was finally sentenced, on August 24, 1981, his attorney called two psychiatrists to the stand. The judge interrupted the second witness, declaring that it was too late to mount an insanity defense. This was a sentencing hearing, and Chapman's guilt was already established. The courtroom burst into applause, despite Jonathan Marks' insistence that his client didn't really comprehend why he'd been brought to court.

When Judge Edwards asked Chapman if he wished to speak, the defendant read a passage from *The Catcher in the Rye*:

> Anyway, I keep picturing all these little kids playing some game in this big field of rye and all.... And I'm standing on the edge of some crazy cliff. What I have to do, I have to catch everybody if they start to go over the cliff.... That's all I'd do all day. I'd just be the catcher in the rye and all. I know it's crazy, but that's the only thing I'd really like to be.

When the defendant was done, the judge told the court,

I disagree with the defense attorney's suggestion that it is an insane crime, an act of a person who is insane. It may well not be a crime committed for the classic motives, revenge or for money, but it was... a crime contemplated, planned and executed by an individual fully aware of the situation and the consequences of his conduct.

There is no question, in this court's judgment, that the defendant may benefit from psychiatric attention, although— equally beyond any possible challenge—there is no doubt... that he is to be held accountable for his knowing, voluntary and intelligent act.

Nonetheless, it appeared that the judge might have been considering Chapman's mental state in imposing a sentence of twenty years to life behind bars—slightly less than the maximum of twenty-five to life. Chapman was ordered to serve his time in Attica, the same prison Lennon had sang about on his record *Some Time in New York City*.

Chapman would later contend that he was fairly happy serving time at the maximum-security facility. "It's not the same prison as it was those years ago," he'd tell Larry King. "I'm treated humanely... I'm not beaten or tortured... Each prisoner in Attica has his own cell. That's one of the good things about Attica."

He also characterized theories that he'd been commissioned to kill by the CIA as "hogwash.... They probably wished they would have had me... but they didn't. It was me doing it. It wasn't them."

■　■　■

In the months following the murder, Yoko was beset with depression and mistrust. When she invited former Deputy Mayor Edward Morrison to the Dakota to discuss her security concerns, she refused to speak about sensitive subject matter out loud, scribbling down her thoughts in note form. "She came into a situation where she heard voices all over, and everyone was spying on her, trying to eavesdrop on her," Morrison said. "It became a very difficult proposition to be with her for any length of time."

With Morrison's assistance, Sanford Garelick, the former city council president and chief of New York's Transit Police, arranged for a security sweep of the Lennon residence. Although specific listening devices were never found, it turned out that Yoko's paranoia was rooted, at least partially, in truth. In 1982, John's personal assistant, Frederic Seaman, was found guilty of grand larceny for stealing the ex-Beatle's diaries, along with letters, contracts, demo tapes, drawings, and stereo equipment. Seaman's "research"—detailing the couple's alleged spending, sex life, and culinary tastes, among other personal affairs—later appeared in a book entitled *The Last Days of John Lennon: A Personal Memoir.*

This, after agents of the U.S. government had conspired to deport John Lennon, and Yoko had watched a stalker murder her husband.

Sean also struggled. When a magician performed at his birthday party the following year, the boy mentioned to Yoko that he wanted the man to teach him incantations to bring John home. "My life from five to six was crazy," Sean told *People.* "I went into a reverse metamorphosis. Instead of growing and turning into something better, I sort of crawled into myself. . . . We got weird letters. Psychotic people were sitting outside our door, thinking they were reincarnates of my father. There were bodyguards everywhere. I don't know how I got through it."

In England, the repairs that John had made in his relationship with Julian began to unstitch. Without fresh, positive memories, Julian could only dwell on his opinions about being overlooked for much of his childhood. Twenty-five years after John was killed, Julian issued a statement, attempting to describe his "very mixed feelings":

"He was the father I loved who let me down in so many ways."

■　■　■

In the wake of the murder, Paul found it difficult to focus in the studio. Fearful of becoming the next assassinated Beatle, he also shied away from playing in public. This was a problem for Wings bandmate Denny Laine, who subscribed to McCartney's earlier philosophy that a group needed the live concert experience to grow. In 1981, Wings disbanded after a decade—a residual casualty of Mark David Chapman.

Before Laine departed, he participated in the recording of "All Those Years Ago," with Paul and Linda. Ringo had already laid down the drum track for the tune, scheduled for release on George's long-delayed album, *Somewhere in England*. After John died, though, Harrison altered the lyrics to work out his conflicted feelings about Lennon—and perhaps apologize to him in the afterlife: "Deep in the darkest night / I send out a prayer to you."

Paul would also release his own tribute—without the assistance of the other Beatles—in 1982, on *Tug of War*, his first LP since the dissolution of Wings. In addition to the highly acclaimed duet with Stevie Wonder, "Ebony and Ivory," the album featured the song "Here Today," about an imaginary conversation between John and Paul. While Lennon claims that the duo were always "worlds apart," McCartney replies that he remembers "how it was before, and I am holding back the tears no more."

Yoko appeared to be most touched by Elton John's memorial, "Empty Garden." When Elton performed the song at Madison Square Garden in August, 1982, both Yoko and the entertainer's godson, Sean, joined him on stage: "And with every drop that falls / We hear your name."

In 1995, all four Beatles played together again, when George, Paul, and Ringo reworked "Real Love," a version of a song John had recorded in six takes in 1979, as well as another incomplete Lennon tune, "Free as a Bird." In 1996, the digital reunion brought the Beatles their last Top 40 single in the United States—twenty-six years after their breakup and sixteen years after their most celebrated member was gunned down.

EPILOGUE

As time passed, George appeared to ease off on security. Although his estate was protected by electronic gates, infrared sensors, and a boundary of razor wire—as well as an alarm system linked to the local police station—neighbors noticed broken fences and overgrowth where trespassers could hide. For a period, dogs patrolled the grounds but, after a while, the ritual stopped. Teenagers occasionally sneaked into the gardens and partied there.

"They have to be seen to be believed," one young man told *The Guardian*.

In 1996, George contacted detectives after a succession of death threats—but that was par for the course with the Beatles, particularly in the post-Lennon era. Then, at approximately 3:20 A.M. on December 30, 1999, Olivia Harrison woke up her husband, claiming to have heard shattering glass. Initially, she wondered if a chandelier had fallen in another room. But soon she detected the unmistakable sound of footsteps. While Olivia phoned police, George went downstairs to investigate.

In the kitchen, George found a broken window, as well as a wing from a statue of St. George that stood on the grounds. The smell of cigarette smoke wafted through the air. He shouted to his wife that there was an intruder on the premises, and rushed back upstairs. From the gallery overlooking the main hall, George spotted thirty-three-year-old Michael "Mad Mick" Abram of Liverpool. According to the psychiatrists who'd later examine him, the former heroin addict was convinced that George had somehow possessed his soul.

Harrison noticed a knife, as well as the sword from the St. George statue, in the man's hand.

"You get down here!" Abram demanded, glaring up at his prey.

"Who are you?"

"You know! Get down here!"

Hoping to distract the unwanted visitor, Harrison began to chant: "Hare Krishna, Hare Krishna...."

Abram charged up the staircase, and George lunged at him, attempting to wrest away the knife. "We fell to the floor," George would testify. "I was fending off blows with my hands. He was on top of me, and stabbing down at my upper body."

Olivia came up behind Abram, smashing him repeatedly with a poker from the fireplace. Crazed, Abram went after Olivia, digging his fingers into her throat.

The fight continued into a cushion-layered section of the mansion that the Harrisons used as a meditation area. Blood splattered on walls and carpet as Abram again stabbed George. Harrison felt his strength draining. One of Abram's seven successful knife thrusts collapsed his target's lung.

"I could hear my lung exhaling, and had blood in my mouth," the ex-Beatle said. "I believed I had been fatally stabbed.... We were going to be murdered."

Olivia refused to accept this option, picking up a Tiffany lamp and swinging it at the attacker. He grabbed the cord and tried to wrap it around her neck. Olivia threw the lamp at Abram and ran downstairs. Abram shifted his attention back to George—hitting him over the head with the object—then took off after Olivia. Bleeding profusely, Abram collapsed on the balcony. Police found him there, and placed him under arrest.

Unlike Chapman, "Mad Mick" was determined to be certifiably insane. He was remanded to a mental health facility, but released in 2002, after apparently "responding well to treatment."

What few people realized was that, at the very moment George was attacked, he was already in a life-and-death struggle with cancer—a disease he attributed to the nicotine habit he'd never been able to overcome. On November 29, 2001, he passed away in Los Angeles.

His body was cremated, and, according to Hindu custom, the ashes released in India's Ganges River. "He had the view," his sister, Louise told *People*, "that his spirit had his body on loan."

On the one-year anniversary of his death, the Concert for George was held at the Royal Albert Hall. Proceeds went to George's Material World Foundation, which supported such charities as Amnesty International, the Downs Syndrome Association, AIDS Crisis Trust, National Society for Autistic Children and World Wildlife Fund.

Paul and Ringo played at the event—McCartney's highlight was his rendition of George's "Something" on ukulele—with none of the conflict or controversy that once surrounded the Beatles. In fact, Paul and Yoko had even teamed up, presenting art exhibitions in both London and New York. In 2008, when Paul and Dave Grohl from the Foo Fighters sang "Band on the Run" together, as part of festivities involving Liverpool's designation that year as the European Capital of Culture, both Yoko and Olivia Harrison attended the show.

■ ■ ■

Julian Lennon's musical career started strong. In the United States, his 1984 debut album, *Valotte*, yielded two Top 10 singles—the title track and "Too Late for Goodbyes." Although he never achieved the same level of success, his songs "Stick Around" and "Now You're in Heaven," in 1986 and 1989 respectively, each hit #1 on the Album Rock Tracks chart.

When Sean entered the family business, the warm feelings between the siblings intensified. "On the occasions that we do see each other, whether it's in England, whether it's in Japan... because he's out on the road from time to time with his own band, it's always like long-lost brothers," Julian told the *Austin*

Chronicle in 1999. "I have a great amount of love for him." Despite evading conversations about John's estate and other volatile topics, Julian contended, "Our love is very clear and very open for one another, aside from all the bull and the stuff in between, which I don't think we need to talk about."

For a period of time, Julian left the music industry, producing and narrating the hypnotic documentary *WhaleDreamers* in 2006, about the tribal culture of whales and the mammals' link to ancient civilizations around the world. Then, while working on a new album, *Everything Changes*, Julian had an epiphany about his father.

The process began when he heard that his childhood friend, Lucy O'Donnell—the inspiration behind "Lucy in the Sky with Diamonds"—was struggling with lupus. Julian hadn't seen his old classmate—now known as Lucy Vodden—since he'd transferred to a different school after his parents' divorce. Out of nowhere, he contacted Lucy at her home in Surrey, in southeast England, to wish her well. Once they'd reconnected, he discovered that they both shared a passion for gardening, and sent her vouchers to allow her to pursue the pastime further.

Oddly, Lucy's association with the song had not been pleasant for her. "As a teenager, I made the mistake of telling a couple of friends at school that I was the Lucy in the song, and they said, 'No, it's not you. My parents said it's about drugs,'" she told the Associated Press. "And I didn't know what LSD was at the time, so I just kept it quiet, to myself."

Lucy's battle with lupus was a prolonged one, lasting five years, and Julian attempted to cheer her up by sending flowers and text messages. But on September 28, 2009, she died. The next month, Julian released a tribute song, a duet with James Scott Cook, whose own grandmother—also named Lucy—happened to be living with the disease. A share of the proceeds from the tune, "Lucy," was directed toward lupus research.

While composing the song, Julian thought about the antagonism he'd been directing at John. "I realized if I continued to feel anger and bitterness toward my dad, I would have a cloud over my head," he told Asian News International (ANI). Because of Lucy, the acrimony dissipated.

Along with everyone else, he could now celebrate John Lennon and the Beatles.

■   ■   ■

In prison, Chapman tried healing his own venomous wounds, working as a porter, "kitchen man," and law library clerk, while renewing his dedication to the Christian path he'd first attempted to walk in high school. "Through my life, off and on, I have struggled with different things, as we all do, and at those times, I would turn to the Lord," he explained to Larry King. "The night of the death of John Lennon, I was far from him. I wasn't listening to him."

But Chapman's God was merciful: "He doesn't condone what I did....He didn't like all the pain I caused everybody, especially John's widow. But...the Lord has a tender spot for prisoners.... I've been leaning on a crutch, but it's a crutch made out of a cross."

Through faith—as opposed to medication or counseling— Chapman claimed to have achieved clarity. "I'm better now," he informed King. "I'm normal." As part of his spiritual restoration, he wrote a letter to J. D. Salinger, apologizing to the author for so publicly invoking the name of *The Catcher in the Rye*.

"I have learned more about people," the gunman would tell authorities. "I know how valuable people are now in the eyes of the Lord. Life is to be taken seriously. It is not a game....I took away one of God's creatures."

Incredibly, Gloria remained committed to her husband, visiting him in Attica for conjugal visits twice a year in a home on the grounds of the penitentiary. If he ever were released, Chapman told officials, he hoped to form a ministry with his spouse: "I really want to go place to place...church to church, and tell people what happened to me, and point them the way to Christ."

Yet his demons lingered behind. Once Chapman broke precedent by murdering a celebrity, the door could no longer be closed. On March 30, 1981, John Hinckley, Jr., fired a .22-caliber revolver six times at Ronald Reagan—wounding the president; press secretary James Brady; Washington, D.C. police officer Thomas Delahanty; and Secret Service agent Timothy McCarthy—specifically to impress actress Jodie Foster. The next year, Arthur Richard Jackson—a stalker from Aberdeen, Scotland—attacked actress Theresa Saldana in front of her California home, nearly taking her life by stabbing her ten times. In 1991, actress Rebecca Schaeffer answered her door and was fatally gunned down by Robert Bardo—an obsessed fan who'd written to Chapman in prison and tried following his example by reading *The Catcher in the Rye*.

Through it all, Chapman became what officials called an "exemplary inmate." He now showed apparent empathy, contending, "I've come to grips with the fact that John Lennon was a person. This has nothing to do with being a Beatle or a celebrity or famous. He was breathing, and I knocked him right off his feet.... I don't have a leg to stand on because I took his from right out under him, and he bled to death. And I'm sorry that ever occurred."

In spite of this, his parole requests were denied every time—and Yoko refused to entertain the thought of forgiving him.

Chapman purportedly understood the way that she felt. "I've thought about what it's like in her mind to be there that night, to hear the screams, to be up all night with Beatle music playing through her apartment window," he said at a 2000 parole hearing. "I've tried to think about what it would be like if somebody harmed my family, and there's just no way to make up for that. And if I have to stay in prison for the rest of my life for that one person's pain...I will."

And he has—notwithstanding the argument that someone convicted of a lesser-known murder would have long ago been released back into society.

■ ■ ■

Following John's death, Officer Peter Cullen passed the sergeant's exam, then went on to become a lieutenant. After he retired to Naples, Florida, he and the 20th Precinct cops from his era continued to meet once a year, often at the Waterfront Crab House in Long Island City, Queens. As a rule, they tended not to mention the death of John Lennon.

"Every generation has their own big thing," he said. "We had John Lennon. Then, after I retired, 9/11 came—and nothing compares to that. I get more questions about John Lennon where I live in Florida because they're celebrity-starved."

In 2004, Ken Dashow—by then a deejay at New York classic rock station Q104.3—devoted an entire Sunday morning shift to commemorating the fortieth anniversary of the Beatles' first visit to the United States. The endeavor was so successful that his program director, Bob Buchmann, asked Ken to try a Beatles show the next week.

"There were even more phone calls, more e-mails," Ken said. "People e-mailing each other. So Bob told me, 'Why don't you do it until I tell you to stop?'"

Very quickly, *Breakfast with the Beatles* became a staple of the New York airwaves. "I can be encyclopedic about it, talk about the twelfth cut of this track, but I don't think that's the magic of it," Ken explained.

> The magic is what the song means to the listener. On Sundays, I have kids under ten listening to the show—the first song they always like is "Yellow Submarine." Everybody has a story—a girl named Loretta who was teased until "Get Back" came out and the Beatles used her name in a song, a father and son who weren't speaking to each other, but came together over the Beatles.
>
> That to me is the magic.

Thirty years after the murder—and three mayoral administrations later—eighty-five-year-old Ed Koch also remained excited by the sound of a Beatles song on the radio. "They made us feel bubbly," he laughed, "champagne-like. I still love to hear McCartney. His voice is gone, but who cares?"

■ ■ ■

In death, John Lennon has truly become a mythical personality. His image was set in bronze in Havana, where President Fidel Castro unveiled the statue to the revolutionary Beatle in 2000. The republic of Abkhazia, a disputed wedge of land in what once was the Soviet Union, has issued two John Lennon stamps. There's a John Lennon Museum in Japan's Saitama Super Arena. And, in 2002, the airport in John's home city—serving nearly six million passengers a year—was renamed "Liverpool John Lennon Airport."

Its slogan: "Above us only sky."

There's even a minor planet named after John—along with asteroids for George, Paul, Ringo, Jerry Garcia, Eric Clapton, Carlos Santana, and Frank Zappa.

If John were still alive, he "would have been terribly upset" by the wars in Iraq and Afghanistan, Yoko has noted, along with the health and ecological crises attributed to greenhouse gas emissions. The creation of the Imagine Peace Tower—on Videy Island, near Reykjavik, Iceland—was Yoko's effort to address both the issues of global peace and global warming. Starting in 1981, Yoko had been gathering more than 700,000 written "peace wishes" from people. These were buried beneath the tower—containing fifteen searchlights powered by a geo-thermal energy grid and reflecting off prisms into the night sky, frequently penetrating the cloud cover. On the base of the white stone monument, the words "Imagine Peace" were carved in twenty-four languages, including Chinese, Arabic, Tamil, Swahili, Tibetan, and Inuktitut. Since 2007, the "tower of light" has shone from October 9, John's birthday, until December 8, the anniversary of the shooting—the unofficial "John Lennon season" for those who share the values espoused by the late Beatle's widow.

"We are here together, billions of us, standing at the dawn of a new age, determined to shift the axis of the world to health, peace, and joy," she said at the 2009 lighting. "I know that John is with us, too. . . . Let's send light to each other and say, 'I love you.'"

With John gone, Sean became Yoko's most constant supporter— a socially cognizant young man harboring distinct ideas about how to direct his musical talents.

"I got a gift that I wasn't expecting," she told the *New York Press* shortly after the album's release. "That gift is to be alive and well at seventy-six. I see all these friends of mine who say, 'I'm going to be forty. I don't know what to do.' And I say, 'Wait until another thirty or forty years, and you're going to feel much better.'"

Still, Yoko never fully recovered from the events of December 8, 1980. For the next three decades, she'd find herself reaching in the darkness for John Winston Ono Lennon, missing the love he gave her and transferred to the universe.

ACKNOWLEDGMENTS

When Backbeat Books editor Mike Edison called, I thought he just wanted to hang out.

But Mike was thinking about the events of December 8, 1980, and had the impression that I could tell the moment-by-moment story he envisioned.

I remember December 8, 1980, vividly, not quite believing the initial news report—why would someone kill a Beatle, especially now, when John Lennon had become such a tranquil figure?—then becoming swept up in the mania that consumed the city. John's death hit everyone hard, but we took it even more personally in New York. The next several days are a blur in my memory, culminating with the crisp imagery of the 100,000 or so faces surrounding me at the Central Park memorial. A week or so later, I was walking into a diner in Queens when I spotted two of those faces, paying the bill at the register.

I nodded at them, and they nodded at me. None of us felt the need to utter a word.

We knew.

I believe that the story of December 8, 1980, is the story of everyone who experienced that sad, unfathomable day. I knew the story so well, yet, in probing it, I wanted to know more.

It was a hard story to relive, and an easy book to write.

Friends came forward to offer their own stories about the day John Lennon died. Others—like Michael Alex, Larry Jaffe, "Leaping" Lanny Poffo, and Chris Policano—helped direct me to players in the drama.

Besides Mike Edison, it felt like the entire Backbeat Books staff lined up behind me—from group publisher John Cerullo to associate editor Bernadette Malavarca to copy editor Sarah Gallogly to Diane Levinson and Aaron Lefkove in publicity.

As always, my foremost appreciation goes to my family: my kids, Dylan and Summer, and my wife, Jennifer Berton Greenberg, who all but staged a Bed-In to support the project, discussing Beatles trivia at the kitchen table, watching Yoko Ono videos on YouTube, and taking the initiative toward creating our own version of *Double Fantasy*.

SELECTED BIBLIOGRAPHY

So much has been written about the life and death of John Lennon, and this bibliography is by no means a complete record of the myriad sources consulted for this book. Nonetheless, in addition to firsthand interviews, the sources listed below were key in the development of the text and suggest the substance and range of material used to research this project.

Books

Baird, Julia. *The Private John Lennon: The Untold Story from His Sister*. Berkeley, CA: Ulysses Press, 2008.

The Beatles. *The Beatles Anthology*. San Francisco: Chronicle Books, 2000.

Brown, Peter, and Steven Gaines. *The Love You Make: An Insider's Story of the Beatles*. New York: New American Library, 2002.

Dogget, Peter. *You Never Give Me Your Money*. London: The Bodley Head, 2009.

Edwards, Henry, and May Pang. *Loving John: The Untold Story*. New York: Warner Books, 1983.

Harrison, George. *I, Me, Mine*. San Francisco: Chronicle Books, 2007 (reissued).

Jones, Jack. *Let Me Take You Down: Inside the Mind of Mark David Chapman, the Man Who Killed John Lennon*. New York: Villard, 1992.

Lennon, Cynthia. *A Twist of Lennon*. New York: Avon Books, 1980.

Lennon, John. *In His Own Write*. New York: Simon & Schuster, 2000 (reissued).

Marshall, William, and Allan Williams. *The Man Who Gave the Beatles Away*. New York: Macmillan, 1975.

Rodriguez, Robert. *Fab Four FAQ 2.0: The Beatles' Solo Years, 1970–1980*. New York: Backbeat Books, 2010.

Salinger, J. D. *The Catcher in the Rye*. New York: Little Brown and Company, 1991 (reissued).

Thompson, Gordon. *Please Please Me: Sixties British Pop, Inside Out*. Oxford and New York: Oxford University Press, 2002.

Newspapers and Magazines

Carter, Imogen. "John Lennon, the Boy We Knew." *The Observer*. December 13, 2009.

Cott, Jonathan. "The Rolling Stone Interview: John Lennon and Yoko Ono." *Rolling Stone*. December 5, 1980.

Denberg, Jody. "Not-So-Primal Therapy." *Austin Chronicle*. August 23, 1999.

Doggett, Peter. "The Day John Lennon, Husband and Friend, Died." *The Times* (UK). September 10, 2009.

Doyle, Patrick, Robert Lane, and Hugh Bracken. "John Lennon Shot Dead Outside Dakota." *New York Daily News*. December 9, 1980.

Fettman, Eric. "She Shows Sean Where Dad Was Shot." *New York Post*. December 11, 1980.

Hamill, Pate. "A Long Night's Journey into Day." *Rolling Stone*. June 5, 1975.

Littlefield, Alex. "Yoko Ono (The Perennial One)." *New York Press*. December 23, 2009.

Maryman, Richard. "Paul McCartney Speaks About the Beatle Breakup and His New Life." *Life*. April 16, 1971.

Montgomery, Paul L. "Police Trace Twisted Path Leading to Lennon's Slaying at Dakota." *New York Times*. December 10, 1980.

Murphy, Tim. "60 Minutes with Yoko Ono and Sean Lennon." *New York*. November 13, 2009.

Sheff, David. "Playboy Interview: John Lennon and Yoko Ono." *Playboy*. January 1981.

Sheff, Vicki. "The Day the Music Died." *People*. December 19, 1990.

Websites

BBC.com

The Beatles Facebook Fan Club of the World

CNN.com

Fabfourfaq.com

Imaginepeace.com

MSNBC.com

Spinner.com

TruTV.com

INDEX